Development and Democracy in Zimbabwe

SOUTHERN AFRICA REGIONAL INSTITUTE FOR POLICY STUDIES (SARIPS)

PUBLIC POLICY SERIES
Series Editor: Ibbo Mandaza

Titles in this Series
Development and Democracy in Zimbabwe
John Mw Makumbe, 1998

Aspects of Development Administration in Zimbabwe
Ibbo Mandaza (forthcoming)

John Mw Makumbe
Development and Democracy in Zimbabwe

SAPES Books
HARARE

First published 1998
SAPES Books
P.O. Box MP 111
Mount Pleasant
Harare

© SAPES Trust and the Author 1998

Typeset and Originated by Southern Africa Printing and Publishing House (SAPPHO), (Pvt.) Ltd.

Printed by Jongwe Press

ISBN   1-77905-042-9

Contents

Acknowledgements

I am deeply grateful to the Department of Political Science and the African Studies Centre at Michigan State University, USA, for providing the necessary facilities for the preparation of this work during my Visiting Scholarship with them. I am also grateful to the Centre for International and Comparative Studies at The University of Iowa, who made it possible for me to stay in the USA for the duration of the preparation of this study. My research assistants in the University of Zimbabwe's Department of Political and Administrative Studies: Kudakwashe, Chipo, Kudzanai, Kwadzanai, Tracy, Gordon, Taurayi, and Lois all deserve special mention for the brilliant work they did meeting with focus groups and traversing the countryside in all forms of rural transport just to make this study possible. The study is part of a five country study of decentralisation which was funded by The Ford Foundation. I am indebted to my colleagues in the team for the many ideas we exchanged, as well the Foundation for facilitating this work. Finally, my gratitude goes to my three lovely girls: Tapiwanashe, Rumbidzai and Virginia, who were my constant companions and provided much needed diversion from this study in order to preserve my sanity.

List of Tables

Abbreviations

AAB	African Advisory Board
AC	African Council
APAs	African Purchase Areas
CAs	Communal Areas
CG	Central Government
DC	District Council
DDC	District Development Committee
ESAP	Economic Structural Adjustment Programme
LAA	Land Acquisition Act
LG	Local Government
LGPO	Local Government Promotion Officer
LGUs	Local Government Units
LHC	Lancaster House Constitution
LSCF	Large Scale Commercial Farm
MLGRUD	Ministry of Local Government, Rural and Urban Development
NGOs	Non-Governmental Organisations
NIPO	New International Political Order
PA	Provincial Administrator
PC	Provincial Council
PDC	Provincial Development Committee
PDSP	Pilot District Support Project
PG	Provincial Governor
PMD	Prime Minister's Directive
RAs	Resettlement Areas
RC	Rural Council
RDC	Rural District Council
RDDC	Rural District Development Committee
SAP	Structural Adjustment Programme
SSCF	Small Scale Commercial Farm
TTLs	Tribal Trust Lands
UC	Urban Council
UDI	Unilateral Declaration of Independence
UZ	University of Zimbabwe
VIDCO	Village Development Committee
WADCO	Ward Development Committee

Abbreviations (cont.)

ZANU (Ndonga)	Zimbabwe African National Union (Ndonga)
ZANU/PF	Zimbabwe African National Union/Patriotic Front
ZAPU/PF	Zimbabwe African People's Union/Patriotic Front
ZG	Zimbabwe Government
ZNA	Zimbabwe National Army

1
Development and Democracy in Zimbabwe

Introduction

The end of the Cold War and the collapse of socialism as an ideology in Eastern Europe, the deteriorating standard of living in most Third World countries, and the growing trend towards plural politics, democracy and participatory development in many African countries require that a re-examination of some of the hitherto unquestioned components of good governance be undertaken. It is largely agreed that decentralisation is one such component, which has the potential to facilitate, or at least enhance, both participatory development and democratic governance in developing countries. But for most of Africa, the state has not always operated in the manner commonly associated with its development in other parts of the world.

The state in Africa has largely been privatised or personalised by incumbent rulers to the extend that decentralisation, however defined, has meant very little empowerment of the people at the local levels - the grassroots. Rather, decentralised structures have, essentially, become a political resource to be used for the benefit of the ruling elite. Even for late starters in the decolonisation race such as Zimbabwe, the wealth of lessons and experiences of other countries does not seem to have resulted in the evolution of a local government system which effectively diffuses power and facilitates the people's participation in the planning and implementation of local development and governance activities. Both democracy and national development do not seem to have benefited from the attainment of national independence, except for the new rulers themselves, who now face the wrath of the people denied the fruits of their independence by an oligarchy which seems to place the people's interests well below theirs in the name of the state, stability and national unity.

This is a study of the impact of decentralisation on the political process in Zimbabwe. The study seeks to determine the effect of decentralisation on democratic rule in this mildly 'revolutionary' regime type, former British colony. Other elements of the decentralisation process, such as administrative, economic and local development performance will only be discussed in relation to their relevance to the impact of decentralisation on democratic governance. The study is based on the premise that, to *the extent that post-*

independence decentralisation was primarily purposed to facilitate the creation of a one-party, socialist state, it has not resulted in the evolution of meaningful democratic governance in Zimbabwe. Indeed, the pillars of the local government system in Zimbabwe today - the Prime Minister's Directives of 1984 and 1985, and the Rural District Councils Act (1988) - were fashioned with this primary objective long before the international demise of so-called scientific socialism. Although minor amendments have since been made to some of these documents, they remain the cornerstones of local government and, therefore, of decentralisation in Zimbabwe.

Methodology

Survey Target Areas

According to the 1984 Prime Minister's Directive on Decentralisation and Development, the basic unit of organisation in Zimbabwe is the Village Development Committee (VIDCO). The Vidco is represented by its chairman and secretary on the Ward Development Committee (WADCO) the chairman of which is that ward's representative on the District Council (DC). But because both the Wadco and the Vidco do not have local authority status, or corporate status, the DC is basically the basic unit of devolved authority in Zimbabwe. The unit of analysis for this study is therefore the DC.

The survey conducted for this study focused on seven DCs in five provinces. These are Chipinge and Maungwe in the Manicaland Province, Chivi and Gutu in Masvingo Province, Gwanda, Gokwe and Kadoma in the Matabeleland South, Midlands and Mashonaland West Provinces respectively. The criteria for the selection of these provinces included both political and socio-economic factors, as well as proximity to the capital city, Harare. Only one urban based DC - Kadoma - was included in the survey. Gwanda and Chipinge, whose DC offices are also urban based, in a sense, are basically rural entities in terms of their areas of jurisdiction and the geographic location of the majority of their citizenry.

Chipinge was included in the survey because of its long standing opposition to the incumbent ruling party, and support for Ndabaningi Sithole, the leader of a small opposition party. In the past three national General Elections, the people of Chipinge have consistently voted into Parliament members of the opposition Zimbabwe African National Union (ZANU Ndonga), much to the chagrin of the ruling Zimbabwe African National Union - Patriotic Front (ZANU/PF) party of Robert Mugabe.

Maungwe District, although also in the Manicaland Province, differs from Chipinge in that it largely supports the ruling ZANU/PF party, and was selected because of its economic diversity manifest in the presence of peasant farmers, who reside in the communal areas (CAs), and small-scale commercial farmers. This mix of two slightly divergent socio-economic groups revealed corresponding differences of opinion among the citizens of this district on some of the issues of decentralisation. In the Masvingo Province, Chivi District was selected because it is one of the poorest districts in Zimbabwe. Overcrowded and drought stricken almost every year, Chivi, probably, represents those parts of Zimbabwe in desperate need for socio-economic development. Political representation for this district in the top echelons of power has been very weak. On the other hand, the area has been of significant interest to development oriented non-governmental organisations (NGOs).

Gutu District, also in the Masvingo Province was included in the survey because of its strong political representation in the national executive. One of the Vice Presidents of Zimbabwe hails from this district. A number of Cabinet Ministers and senior bureaucrats also come from this district. A further feature of Gutu District is that it hosts the Mupandawana Growth Point, one of the Zimbabwe Government's (ZG) 'inventions' aimed at 'urbanising' the rural areas in order to curtail the urban drift and facilitate the decentralisation of commerce and industry from major urban centres. Although Gutu also has both CAs and small-scale commercial farms (SSCFs), the divergence of opinion found in the Maungwe District did not readily obtain in Gutu. Factors other than the presence of CAs and SSCFs may account for this deviation, particularly the level of political representation noted above.

In Matabeleland South, Gwanda District was selected because of its role during the 'Dissident War' (1981-87). During this period, the ZG suspended or dissolved virtually all local government activities and institutions because of the war. Some of the most deplorable post-independence atrocities were, allegedly, committed by the Zimbabwe National Army (ZNA) in this district and in other parts of Matabeleland. Indeed, such local government (LG) structures as Vidcos and Wadcos were only introduced in most parts of Matabeleland after the 1987 Unity Accord between Joshua Nkomo, leader of the now defunct Zimbabwe African People's Union-Patriotic Front (ZAPU/PF), and Robert Mugabe of the ruling ZANU/PF.[1] Surprisingly, these are also the districts where the ordinary citizens are still enthusiastic about decentralised structures of LG. They have not yet become disenchanted with the performance of these bodies, unlike in the districts where these institutions have been operating since 1984/85.

The Gokwe District in Midlands Province was selected because of its remoteness from urban centres, and the fact that it is one of the few areas in Zimbabwe which is settled by people from various ethnic backgrounds, and from various parts of the country. The area is fairly successful in terms of agricultural production. Problems of land shortage, which seriously afflict other districts of Zimbabwe, do not seem to be a problem in the Gokwe area. Politically, the district is well represented at the national level. This district has also been targeted for a Pilot District Support Project (PDSP) which is being undertaken by the British Government's Overseas Development Administration. The PDSP has successfully identified some of the major inhibitions facing decentralised institutions in Zimbabwe. The relevance of the work of the PDSP to this present study needs no further justification.

Finally, as noted earlier, Kadoma District in the Mashonaland West Province is an urban-based DC which is significantly richer than all the other districts included in the study. Located some 140 kilometres away from the capital city, Kadoma was accepted as distant enough to warrant inclusion since it is located in one of the most prosperous provinces of Zimbabwe. Receiving generally good rainfall most years, Kadoma is unique in this study because it does not currently have any resettlement areas (RAs). This is important because of the significant differences between district councils (DCs) and rural councils (RCs) before the two were merged into Rural District Councils (RDCs) recently. RCs used to be white enclaves responsible for the local needs and serving the interests of white commercial farmers, while DCs were relics of the colonial LG system operating in CAs for the benefit of peasant farmers. The amalgamation of RCs and DCs was still in process at the time of this study. Special problems are claimed to be associated with the exercise, which has received considerable resistance from white commercial farmers since the promulgation of the RDCs Act in 1988.

Survey Target Groups and Methods

Structured and unstructured interviews were conducted among focus groups of five to eight citizens at the grassroots - village and ward - levels. A few key individuals were also interviewed at these levels, particularly former civil leaders and political party. Interviews were also conducted with DC elected and appointed officials, and District Administration officers. Most of the field work for this study was undertaken before the amalgamation of RCs and DCs had been implemented. As far as was possible, interviews with officials were held individually rather than in groups. Although this tended to be time-consuming, it also resulted in more diverse opinions from these officials than would have been possible in small groups.

At the provincial level, interviews were conducted with the Provincial Administrators, and selected members of their staff. Provincial Governors and Members of Parliament were largely elusive and the study made use of press reports, official statements and other documentary evidence to gather information about the views of relevant politicians on selected aspects of the study. Members of the Provincial Council were also interviewed but the majority of them tended to respond to items of the interview in relation to the districts they represented at the provincial level. Members of civil society groups were among the most enthusiastic to participate in this study. For the most part, however, the majority of them also tended to be representatives of their various villages and wards in the DCs. Their most useful tool in assessing whether an official or a LG structure was important or useful seemed to be based on whether it "brought development" or not. Democratic governance was generally seen as less significant than development.

Limitations

As noted above, the most significant problem faced by the study was that politicians appeared to be reluctant to be interviewed for this study. The major reason for this was the sour relations between the ZG and the University of Zimbabwe (UZ) staff and students as a result of, *inter alia*, the disturbances of 1990 to 1992. The passing of the University of Zimbabwe (Amendment) Act (1990) seriously damaged the relations between the ZG and the UZ to the extent that some politicians considered it a liability to be interviewed by UZ staff and students on any subject.

Field work was also constrained by the transition nature of most LG units. The ZG was in the process of finalising the amalgamation of RCs and DCs, and provincial and district administration officials prevaricated on some of the aspects of the interviews on the basis that the situation obtaining then could radically change after amalgamation. The study was undertaken at a time when Zimbabwe, like many other African states, was at the crossroads of choosing between the anachronistic one-party system of governance and plural politics or democracy. This was also the time the ruling party was facing significant challenges to its monopoly on power, and opposition political parties were being formed all over the country. The adoption of the economic structural adjustment programme (ESAP), with the attendant rising cost of living, made elements of this study even more sensitive in a political and self-preservation way for some of the target groups and individuals. It is, however, equally correct to state that some of the responses made by the target groups and individuals were of a better quality than would have been the case had the study been undertaken, say, three years earlier.

Synthesis

This study was undertaken concurrently with another study which focused on local government reforms in Zimbabwe. The present study thus, benefited considerably from information obtained through field research for the other study. The information gathered and analysed enables this study to conclude that decentralisation has had very limited impact on the political processes in Zimbabwe. It has not resulted in the evolution of meaningfully democratic nor participative governance. Conceived as it was, during the period when the ruling elite was advocating socialism and the one-party state, decentralisation, or the LG system, was largely modelled along the ruling party's structure and *modus operandi*. The dissipation of the pursuit of both the one-party state and socialism is not congruous with any changes to the format and philosophy of decentralisation espoused prior to 1990. To this end, the study is of the view that, as currently patterned, decentralisation in Zimbabwe serves, mainly, the purpose of protracting the ruling party's tenure of office at the detriment of both participatory development and the evolution of a democratic political system.

2
Theoretical Overview

Definitions

Considerable debate has surrounded the definition of the term "decentralization" to the extent that there is still disagreement among scholars. Rather than contribute to the confusion, this study prefers to accept Mawhood's (1983:2) assertion that a definition is normally accepted more because it is useful than because it is true. Decentralization occurs when national government shares some of its power with other groups, particularly those that are either geographically dispersed, or are responsible for specific functions, or are given jurisdiction over specific physical locations (Mawhood, 1983:4). The key elements in the decentralization process seem to be power, authority and responsibilities, which are diffused in such a way that they flow from the centre to the periphery, or to sections of the periphery, in a manner deliberately decided upon by the centre. Examples include the power to tax, make by-laws and regulations, and to some extent, to raise, spend or to allocate local resources.

Smith (1985:1) distinguishes between mere dispersal of branches of a central government ministry from the capital to the periphery from decentralization, which, according to him, amounts to sub-dividing the state's territory into smaller units and institutions. These are then given power and authority to carry out certain specific political and administrative functions pertaining to their designated areas of jurisdiction or specialization. The organizations and institutions to which central power and authority are transferred may themselves transfer some of their power and authority to lower levels within their designated areas.

Other authorities tend to be more specific on what responsibilities or powers are transferred, and to which levels or agencies they are transferred. Rondinelli and others (1983:13), for example, are of the view that central government and its agencies transfer responsibilities for planning, management, resource raising and allocation to dispersed or field units of the centre, to lower levels of central government, to public authorities or corporations, to regional functional authorities, and to NGOs, voluntary and private sector organizations.

Types of Decentralization

To the extent that decentralization involves the transfer of power, it should follow that such aspects of governance as development, democracy, participation, equality, efficiency, and so on, have a bearing on the concept. These elements are easier to understand after defining the various types of decentralization commonly in use in developing countries. Deconcentration is the transfer of adequate authority for the carrying out of specified functions from central ministries and their agencies to staff of the same ministries or agencies who are situated outside the national headquarters. It is an intra-organizational pattern of power relationships, according to Hyden (1983:85). The idea is that of shifting the work load from officials who are centrally located to their colleagues located outside the capital city as a way of allowing for adjustments to central directives to suit local conditions (Rondinelli et al., 1983:14).

Devolution, unlike deconcentration, is the transfer of 'legally defined elements of political power' to local government units (LGUs) or to specialized or functional authorities (Crook and Manor, 1991:22). The bodies to which such political power is transferred thus have the responsibility to carry out specified or residual functions in their areas of jurisdiction, or pertaining to the provision of goods and services of their specialization. In other words, devolution refers to the an inter-organizational transfer of power from the centre to units outside the normal command structure of central government (Hyden, 1983:85). The functions performed by these local units generally lie outside the direct control of central government (CG) which, nonetheless, maintains indirect supervision and control of these autonomous units (Rondinelli et al., 1983:24).

Delegation, the third type of decentralization commonly used in developing countries, pertains to the transfer of managerial responsibilities, for functions that are specified, from CG to public corporations or parastatals, which normally, lie outside the regular bureaucratic structure. (Gasper, 1991:9). Delegated authority can also be transferred to 'regional development agencies, special function authorities [and] semi-autonomous project implementation units' (Rondinelli et al. 1983:19).

As under devolution, CG does not have direct control over bodies to which delegated authority is granted. It, however, retains ultimate responsibility for these bodies. Arguing that delegation is a form of deconcentration, Crook and Manor imply that the key difference between the two is the separation of the financial and administrative functions of bodies with delegated authority from those of central bureaucracy (1991:22). Most authorities, however, treat delegation as significantly distinct from deconcentration.

The fourth and final type of decentralization is privatization, which occurs when CG divests itself of responsibility for certain functions, or the provision of certain goods and services, and transfers them to, or allows them to be performed or provided by voluntary, private or non-governmental organizations. Privatization also includes CG's transfer of responsibilities and functions to what Rondinelli et al. (1983:28) call 'parallel organizations' These include professional groups, trade associations, political parties, religious groups and co-operatives. In other cases CG transfers responsibilities and functions to groups which represent various interests in society some of which are mentioned above. The key factors in privatization seem to be that the bodies to which these functions or responsibilities are transferred are not necessarily subject to CG control or supervision. Further, the goods and services tend to be provided on the open market, although, in some cases, professional, ethical or moral and other considerations may also be observed by such bodies.

This study is primarily concerned with deconcentration and devolution since these are the two types of decentralization that are more involved with the issue of democratic governance and the evolution of specific political processes. The other two types will only be referred to in relation to the effect they may have on either the first two types, or such related concepts as development, democracy and participation. The idea is not to trivialize privatization and delegation, but to sharpen the study's focus on deconcentration and devolution which necessarily have more significant consequences for democracy and development.

Rationale for Decentralization

This sub-heading is purposed to include elements normally discussed under such headings as the objectives, advantages, benefits or value of decentralization (Rondinelli et al. 1983:9; Otzen et al., 1988:14; Smith, 1985:3). Authorities are largely agreed that, to all intends and purposes, excessive centralization of state power and authority has a debilitating effect on good government. Decentralization, in its various forms, is argued to result in the achievement of higher levels of participation in decision-making, development planning and implementation, and, therefore, in the maintenance of political stability. It facilitates the involvement of a wide variety of groups in the allocation of national resources for development and, thus enhances equity. It also establishes better communication and relations between various levels of government, and between bureaucracy and members of the public. This does not only reduce delays in decision-making, but also allows for the modification of central directives, plans, policies, projects and programmes to suit local conditions, thereby making development more relevant to the needs of the people in various communities.

Decentralization is also argued to be beneficial to central bureaucracy in that it reduces the workload, and therefore, the congestion at the central level. This, in turn, improves the CG's responsiveness to public demands and requests. The quality and quantity of goods and services provided by both the CG and LGUs are expected to improve as a result of decentralization. Since it implies a peripheral location of specific units of government, decentralization is argued to enhance the speed at which problems which arise during the implementation of development programmes are rectified. Because decentralization, necessarily, means that more technical and administrative functionaries than operate at the centre are required, it is claimed to be instrumental in the creation of large numbers of skilled personnel with the relevant responsibilities.

Further, decentralization facilitates the acquisition of more accurate information on conditions or situations obtaining at the periphery, which information can then be used for the planning of more appropriate development and governance activities. The information needed by local decision-makers in order to effectively plan, raise local resources and allocate local and other resources necessarily results in the raising of consciousness about both their locality and the rest of the country. This helps to make centrally planned or initiated programmes better known and supported at the local level, thereby giving such programmes a good chance of success or effectiveness (Rondinelli et al., 1983:9-11).2 Asserting that decentralization brings government closer to the people, Smith (1985:4-5) writes: 'politically, decentralization is said to strengthen accountability, political skills and national integration...it promotes liberty, equality and welfare'. To this end, it facilitates the viability of the local level as an effective training ground for political leadership at both the local and national levels.

Mawhood (1983:9-10), who does not regard deconcentration as a form of decentralization, identifies five characteristics of a decentralized local body by arguing that such a body should have: its own budget; a separate legal existence; authority to allocate resources; a range of different functions; and its decisions are made by the people's representatives. Thus, according to him, 'If one or more of the characteristics are missing, or are only weakly present, it must be asked whether we are looking at a decentralized or only a deconcentrated structure of government.' As stated earlier, for the purpose of this study, however, both deconcentration and devolution are forms of decentralization which differ only in the degree that local elective representatives are allowed to make decisions regarding the functions of the decentralized body. The characteristics noted by Mawhood, nonetheless, remain useful guidelines for understanding the performance of LGUs and other decentralized bodies *vis-a-vis* CG.

Finally, the relationship between democracy and decentralization needs to be explained briefly. Thus, while democracy is not necessarily, part of the definition of decentralization (Crook and Manor, (1991:24), it has considerable influence on the concept and practice of decentralization. For example, as Crook and Manor note, it has a bearing on the level of autonomy, and therefore, on the size of decentralized bodies. To the extent that democracy entails popular participation in local elections, decision-making for development planning and implementation, it has to be seen as an essential ingredient of the process of decentralization. Indeed, democracy at the local level may determine whether decentralized bodies are weak or strong *vis-a-vis* the CG which creates them.

But decentralization also has its problems. Critics of the concept argue that it can be divisive and separatist in character and effect, therefore, a negation of national unity and integration (Smith, 1985:5). Because it requires that goods and services be provided at local rather than national level, it is said to reinforce narrow sectional interests and is, therefore, 'anti-egalitarian' (Smith, 1985:5). At the local level, decentralization is criticized for having the tendency of benefiting certain classes at the expense of the generality of the people. Revolutionary regime types of government in developing countries are, therefore, likely to ensure that decentralized bodies are either limited in their autonomy, or that they have limited local resources to allocate, or that, as in 'mixed authorities,' appointive, rather than elective, officials make the final decisions, or decisions which have the most significant impact upon local development and governance. Decentralization, thus, becomes a mere extension of the national elite's resource and power base, but of dubious utility to the people. Worse still, decentralization can result in the creation of effective institutions of public control at the local level. Finally, for most developing countries which suffer from a shortage of appropriately qualified and trained personnel, decentralization can be argued to result in the provision of goods and services of a poorer quality than may obtain at the central level, where better educated, skilled and experienced personnel are more readily available. Like any other resources, skilled manpower tends to gravitate towards the centre.

Decentralization is, nevertheless, viewed by most governments as an essential component of good government. It is claimed to result in the empowerment of local communities to take charge of their destinies. But decentralization cannot resolve the many problems that developing societies face. It is no panacea for problems of underdevelopment, poverty, squalor, ignorance and disease by itself. Even when it contributes positively to the resolution or alleviation of some of these problems, it only does so within certain parameters that are dictated by factors outside the general purview of decentralization. Within Africa, a number of observations on the practice of decentralization since the end of the colonial era can be made.

General Problems of Decentralization in Africa

The proliferation of authoritarian regimes as a result of military and traditional dictatorships, single-party states and personal rule has been the dominant feature of government and politics in post-colonial Africa. Colonial rule in Africa was authoritarian in nature and in practice, and only utilized decentralization as an effective way of facilitating both control of the "natives" and the collection of badly needed revenue. Decentralization was also an effective weapon or political resource for the colonialists who made use of it to execute the principle of divide and rule, reinforcing ethnic divisions and eroding the notion of nationalism. It was from the ashes of this form of local government, or decentralization, that post-colonial Africa attempted to reconstruct a 'modern' LG system. The odds against the success of constructing a meaningful, acceptable and effective LG system were enormous. The nature or characteristic of the post-colonial LG system must, however, not be blamed only on the colonial legacy of Africa; there have been ample opportunities for African nations to discontinue the inherited LG systems and, indeed, to determine new courses of decentralizing central government since independence.

Several problems have plagued decentralization in post-colonial Africa. The first one is the erosion of local autonomy and the increase of central power and authority over virtually all areas of governance and social endeavour. The second one may be uncertainty over the maintenance of political control (Kasfir, 1983:25), coupled with increasing poverty and other socio-economic ills, which militated against any meaningful diffusion of real power from the centre to the periphery. Thirdly, there has tended to be excessive control of LGUs by the centre, to the effect that the decentralized bodies failed to attract and stimulate local participation (Laleye and Olowu), thereby negating both democratic governance and participative development.

The fourth problem relates to a general reluctance to decentralize the national budget, or allow LGUs to raise local resources for the development of their localities. Instead, CGs have preferred that they do most of the revenue collection activities, and then distribute or allocate some of the resources to LGUs, supposedly, on an equitable basis. Apart from creating a dependency mentality among the citizens of LGUs, this practice has also created the impression that LG is basically impotent, and a waste of time for would-be participants in local governance. Perhaps, the fifth problem is the proliferation of parastatals, most of which are deleterious loss-making national liabilities, resulting in the 'stultification of decentralized local governments and in the strengthening of the role and importance of central government' (Laleye and Olowu).

The sixth is the paucity of skilled manpower at the sub-national levels, mainly as a result of the limited remunerative and other benefits obtaining at these levels vis-a-vis those offered by CG, or in the private sector. This has meant that LGUs have only been able to provide goods and services of mundane quality. Weak systems of accountability, which tended to promote unethical conduct among both elected and appointed local public servants, aggravated the problem of scarcity of local resources for meaningful development. Finally, the fact that civil society is not as well developed in Africa as it is in most developed countries exacerbated the problems surrounding the effectiveness of post-colonial LG development in most of Africa.

Recent developments in Africa have, however, resulted in considerable activities among the grassroots who now demand plural politics, democracy and visible development as opposed to authoritarian and military rule and traditional dictatorships at the national level. The extent to which developments at the national level will be transferred to local levels, and made to influence decentralization policies and practices, still remains to be seen in most countries of Africa. Ruling elites have an inordinate capacity to adapt, or devise new strategies for their own survival. The imposition of structural adjustment programmes and their attendant conditionalities of reduced CG spending, promotion of 'good government,' protection of civil liberties and civil society, and the refocusing (or reduction) of CG's involvement in community or local development have yet to demonstrate their consequence for the nature of decentralization in most of Africa. The so-called receding role of the state may turn out to be a tactical move to gather momentum for the next assault on civil liberties and the dwindling national purse.

A recent study of decentralization in three countries of Sub-Saharan Africa (Green et al., 1991:4-5) makes the following summarized conclusions:

1. Neither control nor influence of central governments have been significantly curtailed;

2. LGUs have substantially enhanced authority to undertake many of the new tasks assigned to them but are limited in their operational capabilities by their restricted access to tax instrumentalities and regulations

imposed by national governments that increase the cost of service delivery;

3. Decentralization (as currently instituted) and structural adjustment programmes [SAPs], singly or in tandem, do not seem to have prompted people to increase investments in productive activities...; and,

4. Politically, citizens are able to hold locally elected officials more accountable for delivering quality public services than in the days before 'decentralization.'

Regrettably, these conclusions are based on only three countries in one region of the African continent. The relevance of most of the conclusions to situations in most other African states can, however, not be disputed. It is doubtful that African CGs will allow their LGUs to operate purely on the basis of their citizens' demands, or in accordance with the wishes of their people. CG's influence over LGUs has significantly damaged the latter in the view of the people, to the extent that the latter is not regarded as connoting local people's participation in development and democratic government.

The second general conclusion noted above attests to the fact that, given the relevant resources, LGUs in African states can execute their designated responsibilities without the need for CG's direct involvement. But the rationale for restricting LGUs' authority to tax or raise local resources goes well beyond CG's interest of being visible at the sub-national level. It is also aimed at ensuring that the centre remains adequately endowed with resources which will enable it to operate some of its activities which may not be credible, or may fail to attract sufficient empathy at the local level. Further, as Kasfir (1983:26) rightly observes, national leaders' reluctance to distribute authority and power to sub-national levels after independence was based on the illusion that they would acquire more power:

> They discovered instead that they had gained the negative power to prevent other political actors from taking independent initiatives, but not the positive power to implement policies that would improve social welfare.

This centralization of national resources results in, inter alia, the obstruction of meaningful political and socio-economic development at the sub-national level, and this has negative, long-term implications for national development as a whole. Its implications for the development of a democratic political system of governance can necessarily be assumed to be negative as well. The resort to 'tools of coercion instead of techniques of persuasion' (Kasfir, 1983:26), so ubiquitous in Africa, is an admission of the futility of continued central control of all the facets of governance at local and national levels, for 'Elasticity of control' undergirds successful decentralization' (Kasfir, 1983:26).

The third conclusion reached by Green *et al* as noted above underscores the debilitating effect of decentralization on the economic development of LGU areas in most African countries. As the discussion of the Zimbabwe case will indicate, CG's efforts at encouraging private enterprises to decentralize their operations to rural areas, because it was not accompanied by, *inter alia*, policies which significantly influenced or promoted genuine local decision-making, generation and allocation of resources, met with only partial, and very limited success. On the whole, rural areas have largely remained underdeveloped and neglected. The basic infrastructure which the CG has provided, sometimes after heavy borrowing from abroad, has not been sufficient to motivate either local or urban-based entrepreneurs to risk their resources by investing in communities which are largely impoverished, and which are not empowered to embark on any socio-economic programmes of their own initiative without CG's approval and funding.

Regarding the fourth and final conclusion noted above, it is, probably fair to observe that, ultimately, citizens are forced to come to the realization that considerably little can be done by the local officials to remedy the problem of delivery of low quality goods and services. A common feature of the insulation of public officials at the local level is their ability to "pass the buck" whenever the people make demands for better goods and services than can be provided from local resources, or from CG's allocation for a given LGU, especially given the austerity measures dictated by SAPs commonly manifest in many African countries. Indeed, Green *et al* (1991:5) admit that local communities' ability to hold LGU elected officials accountable for the poor performance of these bodies is not as meaningful as it should be, were decentralization not afflicted with the various quandaries as noted in this study. Penalizing locally elected officials for LGU deficiencies they have neither the power nor the resources to correct eventually becomes counter-productive for the local communities themselves.

Goran Hyden (1983:88) adds a further dimension to the discussion of Africa's post-colonial centralizing tendencies by arguing that the departure of the colonialists resulted in, *inter alia*, increasing influence exerted on policy-making and governance by the economy of affection and clan politics. Devolved LGUs with effective decision-making and resource raising and allocative powers could, in the new elites' view, have caused various kinds of problems, including the overshadowing of CG authority, power and effectiveness in governance. Further, power struggles between elected and appointed officials at the local level gave CG the excuse it needed to intervene more actively at that level, thereby generating, not only a much needed broader power base, but also providing an avenue for the process of 'departicipation' and 'depoliticization,' common features of political processes in post-colonial Africa.

Both departicipation and depoliticization were aimed at ensuring that power remained only in the hands of the national elites. Their perception of power, according to Balogun (1992:4), essentially, militated against decentralization as defined in this study. They were reluctant to share power with local elites or people's representatives at the local levels:

> Almost invariably, the elites behaved as if a power that was shared was as good as lost. This in a way explains the tendency on the part of central government leaders to pay lip service to the idea of autonomous local government. While acknowledging that the interests of the masses would best be served if development started "from below", the bulk of the decisions taken by the central government often stifled local initiative. No further evidence of ambivalence (on the role of local government) is required than in the allocation of resources and the conferment of power and authority....the central government most frequently expected much from local government, but gave very little in terms of resources and power (Balogun, 1992:4).

But in this, the national elites were not alone; career bureaucrats also adopted subtle techniques aimed at frustrating the effective expression of popular aspirations and curbing local initiative. Balogun (1992:4) asserts that the empire-building tendencies of career bureaucrats often stand in the way of the decentralization of power and the transfer of resources to local levels by the national elites: '...bureaucratic norms (of centralization, hierarchical conformation, professionalization, and standardization) often run counter to the idea of local political control of administrative action.'

This pathological and paternalistic perception of the masses, coming as it does from both the national elites and career bureaucrats, assumes that people cannot lead their own change processes. It reduces the masses to mere objects of change and development. It cannot result in the empowerment of the poor.

Goran Guy (1983:345) aptly states:

> Democratic national politics begins by building up mass-based local government, one that evolves from base/intermediate organizations to councils, that represents citizens and work units. Such local governments would not be looking to improve local social services by handouts from national authorities. Instead the goal would be relative self-reliance by the more creative mobilization of local citizen initiatives. A reasonably participatory local society will be ready to project alternative visions of state or regional development and work to create the democratic institutions to carry it out. Several democratically based regional entities can then collaborate on an alternative vision of national development and on the means of its implementation.

To what extent then are the ideals expressed above and discussed in this sub-section obtain in Zimbabwe's local government system? Is it possible that decentralization in post-colonial Zimbabwe has also been viewed as just a means of extending CG's power and authority to the local level? Has there been realistic empowerment of the people at the local level, or has decentralization been reduced to a mobilization mechanism for the effective execution of centrally initiated development and governance programmes and activities? What are the views of the people regarding the process of decentralization in Zimbabwe? Do they feel that they are, indeed, active participants in the democratization of both the political and the developmental processes in Zimbabwe? While this study cannot claim to have comprehensive answers to all of these questions, it is certainly hoped that some light can be shed on the nature of decentralization and the local government system in Zimbabwe. But to do so requires that a brief examination of the local government system under colonial Zimbabwe be undertaken.

3
Decentralisation in Zimbabwe

Selected Features of the Colonial LG System

Zimbabwe's LG system dates back to 1891 when the Salisbury Sanitary Board was established (Wekwete,1988.1:19). The system was primarily based on the principle of 'separate development' of races, notably whites and blacks, with the former benefiting more from the system than the latter as shall be shown in this study. The evolution of the LG system was based on the racial division of land which, through a number of pieces of legislation, created urban areas, which were the preserve of whites (Patel, 1988:20), large-scale commercial farms (LSCFs), which were also settled only by whites, and Tribal Trust Lands (TTLs) and, later, African Purchase Areas (APAs), which were considered African commercial farmlands. Three types of local authorities emerged, namely: urban councils (UCs), rural councils (RCs) in the LSCFs, and African Councils (ACs)[3] catering for blacks in the TTLs and APAs. A brief discussion of each of these three types of LGUs may be appropriate.

Urban Councils (UCs)

Most urban centres were located on land which successive colonial governments had designated as white land, and which was in agro-ecological regions one, two and three. These are areas of good rainfall, temperate climate and relatively more fertile soils. A few urban areas, particularly mining centres, were, however, located in the lowveld which largely falls within regions three and four. Africans were only allowed to reside in urban areas if they were employed in commerce, industry or as domestic workers of white urban dwellers. Colonial period UCs, therefore, evolved along the twin-city concept which separated African from European residential areas. The quality of services and amenities provided by UCs was also racially determined, with those made available to African occupied areas being of considerably lower quality than those intended for white urban citizens.

In terms of decentralization, UCs, which derived their authority from the Urban Councils Act (1973)[4], were more autonomous than ACs. They had authority to make by-laws, collect certain taxes, and rates, and had democratic elections. Their functions included: planning and implementation of development; provision of social and infrastructural services and amenities;

regulation of social and economic activities; and, the raising of local revenue[5].
In order to cater for the needs of urban-based Africans, UCs created African
Advisory Boards (AABs), which had such responsibilities as the provision
and administration of housing, recreational and other social facilities, and the
collection of rentals. AABs were often represented by a white councillor in
the UC.

Rural Councils

The Rural Councils Act (1966) transformed the Road Councils which existed
in most LSCFs into RCs, which used to cater for the interests of white
commercial farmers in rural areas. RCs had authority to levy property taxes,
rates and service charges on their council area members, as well as on
residents, and business enterprises located at urban centres within their areas.
The functions of RCs were basically identical to those of UCs, and they also
had an equal amount of local autonomy. Their resource base was strong and
enabled them to provide a wide range of goods, services and other benefits to
their members, as well as develop their areas.

Although RCs were democratic entities, they lacked mechanisms of
effectively representing the thousands of African farm labourers who resided
in their areas. The fact that the LGU system was based on race and on the
division of land between the two race groups also created a situation which,
to date the ZG is still striving to correct. Most commercial farmland is still in
the hands of white farmers in Zimbabwe. The Land Acquisition Act (LAA)
(1992) is intended to empower the ZG to compulsorily acquire some of the
LSCF land for distribution to landless peasants. The Rural District Councils
Act (1988) was promulgated in order to remove the race factor from the
determination of types of LGUs in the rural areas of the country. There has
been considerable resistance to both these pieces of legislation from white
farmers, but the ZG has already started amalgamating adjacent RCs and DCs.
Further, some seventy LSCFs have been designated for acquisition by the ZG
since the passing of the LAA in 1992.

African Councils

Unlike in the urban and the LSCF areas, local government in the African rural
areas evolved rather slowly. Although suggestions to the effect that local
government be extended to African areas were made as far back as 1923, no
action was taken until 1931 when Native Boards were established after
consultations between Native Commissioners of various districts and chiefs
and headmen (Palley, 1966:659-660). The resultant Native Boards were

headed by the Native Commissioners, with chiefs and headmen being *ex-officio* members. Elected members, whose number would not exceed that of *ex-officio* members, were also included at the discretion of the Native Commissioner. Native Boards were later transformed into Native Councils after the passing of the Native Councils Act (1937). Native Councils were, however, not given any powers to raise local revenue; they were entirely dependent on CG grants, donations and fees. They were, essentially, local or area administration rather than local government.

The successors of the Native Councils, the African Councils were equally impotent even though the Native Commissioners had relinquished their authority as presidents of African Councils. The escalation of African nationalism in the late fifties and early sixties forced the colonial and settler rulers to attempt to galvanize support for white rule from among African traditional leaders - chiefs and headmen. The Tribal Trust Lands Act (1967), for example, restored land allocation powers to traditional leaders in order to obtain their support for the unilateral declaration of independence (UDI) of 1965. The African Law and Tribal Courts Act (1969) restored to traditional leaders, the powers of trying civil and some criminal cases among Africans. In 1973, the African Councils Act was amended to accord traditional chiefs more executive and administrative powers *vis-a-vis* their councils.

These measures were not only being undertaken in order to counteract nationalist support among Zimbabwe's Africans. Rather, they were also intended by the white regime as a way of divesting itself of rural development responsibilities in the African areas. They also relieved the settler regime from having to enforce certain difficult, unacceptable or politically sensitive policies in African areas. Further, the Native Land Husbandry Act of 1951 had created large numbers of landless people, and the colonial administration expected the chiefs to deal with that problem.

The white regime further sought to withdraw itself from involvement in African matters through a provincialization policy, which resulted in the creation of regional authorities under the Regional Authorities Act (1973). Here again, the majority of the members of these authorities were traditional leaders. These bodies were responsible for all administrative activities in the African areas. An attempt was also made to create a separate African public service to operate under Regional Authorities. It was, basically, a form of apartheid through local government. These measures were, however, not particularly successful in creating a viable LG system for Africans in colonial Zimbabwe. These, and many other policy strategies, only served to antagonize the Africans and, therefore, fuel the fires of nationalism.

For example, although District (Native) Commissioners handed over the chairmanship of district councils to elected officials after 1973, they still maintained executive oversight on these bodies and could intervene in all matters as they were still presidents of district councils. Indeed, some of the major targets of the liberation war were district council facilities in all parts of the country. The colonial regimes had successfully alienated the people, not only from their traditional leaders, but also from the practice of local government as they were made to understand it. This explains why the first post-colonial ZG had to engage the services of former guerrillas, especially those who were political commissars in ZANU/PF, as Local Government Promotion Officers (LGPOs). Their task was to "sell" the idea and ideals of local government to the grassroots in Zimbabwe.

In terms of decentralization, it has already been stated that, by and large, the LG system devised by colonial regimes was, essentially, local or field administration. It did not come about as a result of any sincere devolution of authority by central government to district councils. Instead, DCs were basically being used as an effective extension of CG to the African areas. The dominant role played by the chiefs and headmen did not fool the Africans to accept the concept and practice of LG as a viable, just and fair system of self-determination and governance. The limited role played by democratically elected DC officials meant that the people's wishes were not being effectively represented in DCs. The colonial District Commissioner's dominance further indicated to Africans that the existence of DCs was at the pleasure of the white minority regimes of the time. Finally, the fact that African DCs were dependent on CG for their sustenance and had little authority to raise their own resources, necessarily meant that their autonomy was extremely limited, indeed.

Observations on the Colonial LG System

Based, as it was, on two of the most detested features of the colonial era - racism and land alienation - the LG system discussed above had little opportunity of being accepted by Africans, nor had it any prospects of accomplishing what a LG system is normally designed to achieve. The organizational, financial and functional restrictions imposed on the African LGUs reduced them to mere agencies of the loathed white minority regimes in the view of most Africans. Writing mainly about UCs in Zimbabwe, Jordan (1984:89) states:

> The existence of autonomy in local affairs is a *sine qua non* for the continued existence of local democracy. Without it the councils would be empty shells attracting little public

interests or support. Threats to local autonomy can come in two direct forms. Direct interference by central government, as has happened in Zambia and Kenya, or direct interference by ministers or ministries in municipal affairs. But just as inimical to local government is the loss or absence of resources, particularly financial resources, to meet local needs to implement council decisions.

To the extent that African DCs were utilized by the white CG to implement some of its repressive measures against the Africans, they were, rightly, rejected as institutions through which the people could express their opinions, articulate their felt and real needs, and take action to resolve their problems. The use, or abuse, of traditional leaders only served to alienate these leaders from their people.

In its desperate attempt at thwarting the escalating armed struggle, the colonial regime further fragmented DCs in order to ensure that every African chief had a council in his area. There were no less than 220 DCs in Zimbabwe by the time independence was attained in 1980. Very few of these, if any, were operational because of the war (Mutizwa-Mangiza, 1991:55), and because they lacked community support for their very existence. But the small size of the African LGUs further aggravated their non-viability, thereby limiting their chances of demonstrating the advantages of local governance. This is not to argue that the colonial regimes had intended that the LG system among Africans in Zimbabwe was supposed to be a remarkable success. Rather, some of their intentions, as noted earlier, included the facilitation of separate development between whites and blacks, tactical withdrawal of central enforcement or implementation of unpopular policies, as well as alluring Africans away from participating in or supporting the liberation struggle in particular, and African nationalism in general. Mutizwa-Mangiza aptly states: '...the real intention behind their [Native Councils] creation was to counteract independent political organization among indigenous blacks' (1991:54). At the heart of the colonial LG system, this study would argue, was the desperate desire for effective social control of the Africans by their colonial masters. It is ironic that, as shall be argued later, the same principle can be argued to be the primary objective of most of the post-colonial LG reforms as well.

The situation pertaining to both UCs and RCs was, however, very different. Both of these types of LGUs had effective and viable levels of autonomy. They commanded viable quantities (and qualities) of resources, in both financial and personnel terms. They catered for manageable numbers of citizens, given their resource bases. They had a vested interest in the success and perpetuation of the colonial system in Zimbabwe. The colonial CG largely left them to their own devices; its control over them was kept at minimum levels. They were the beneficiaries of both racism and the racially determined land apportionment system, the cornerstones of the LG system in colonial Zimbabwe. But as the war escalated in the 1970s, they, particularly the RCs, began to see the futility of their hopes for the inequitable, unfair and unjust system. The attainment of national independence in 1980, thus, marked the beginning of the end of their privileged position. The correction of past injustices, the demolition of century-old institutions, laws habits and attitudes, however, takes long. Efforts at correcting some of the anomalies of the colonial era are still in progress in Zimbabwe at the time of this study. It is to the post independence LG system that this study now turns.

Post-Colonial Decentralization

Selected LG Reforms Since 1980

The majority of studies so far undertaken on LG reforms in Zimbabwe since 1980 have concentrated on the development planning perspective[6]. Very little has been written and published on the LG system from a political science perspective. This present study will attempt an examination beyond mere development planning, although it must be accepted that the line between political and developmental participation is very blurred, if such a line exists at all. Indeed, it will not be possible for this study to do justice to the topic of democracy in LG in Zimbabwe without drawing heavily from both the developmental and planning dimensions of the system. Thus, to the extent that democracy is not an end in itself, but a means to the ultimate end of local empowerment for collective (and individual) development, any study of decentralization in a developing society such as Zimbabwe, cannot be of much relevance to societal development if it is exclusive of development and related perspectives.

The colonial LG system discussed above, as noted earlier, was repugnant to the majority of Africans in Zimbabwe. It was therefore, logical that on coming to power in 1980, the ZANU/PF government made haste to introduce wide-ranging reforms aimed at removing some of the racial considerations of the colonial regime from the LG system. A number of pieces of colonial legislation were either amended or repealed, and new directives and statutes were issued. These related to the three types of the inherited LG system discussed above. Since considerable details are provided through works undertaken earlier (see note 6 above), this section will focus only on those elements of the reforms that have a bearing on democracy and the evolution of a democratic system of governance in Zimbabwe.

Urban Council Reforms

Post-independence amendments to the Urban Councils Act (1973), Chapter 214 resulted in the democratization of the LG system at that level by removing racial discrimination pertaining to representation and tenure in urban areas (Wekwete, 1988:20). Former local government areas (or African townships) were incorporated into UC areas soon after independence (Jordan, 1984:9). Democratization of the UCs also resulted in the enfranchisement of rent-paying lodgers who did not have the vote under the colonial urban LG system (Helmsing, 1990:101). These amendments were also intended to transform UCs from a twin-city conceptual basis to a one-city one, although there is ample evidence to the effect that, to a large extent, this transformation has not yet been accomplished to date (Wekwete, 1988:21)[7]. Further, although Wekwete argues that the 1980 amendments to the Urban Councils Act sought to enhance the viability of UCs, there is ample evidence, at least, in terms of devolution, that the amendments eroded, somewhat, UCs' autonomy by increasing both administrative and political controls and oversight by the CG:

> Since 1980, there has been a relatively stronger hand from central government, largely to effect socio-political changes. The Minister has also exercised the right to remove an elected Council (Mutare, Gweru) where it was felt the elected officials were not in line with people's wishes (MLGRUD/SALA, 1985:16).[8]

The role of the Minister is also emphasized in relation to elections, powers of borrowing, finance and audit of UCs. To a large extent, however, UCs in post-colonial Zimbabwe are 'largely bureaucracies with limited business orientation' (MLGRUD/SALA, 1985:17). UCs, nevertheless, still remain the local authorities in post-colonial Zimbabwe which have the highest levels of local autonomy.

Party politics have played a significant role in city governance since 1980. Prior to the signing of the Unity Accord between the two major political parties, ZANU/PF and ZAPU/PF in 1987, the council chambers of both Harare and Bulawayo were always dominated by these two parties respectively, with a sprinkling of independent, mainly white, councillors representing low-density areas for most of that period. Only a few Africans had managed to purchase property in low-density areas of major urban areas by 1985.

Recently, newly formed political parties have also made inroads into LG politics. For example, the Mount Pleasant ward of Harare City Council was represented by a University of Zimbabwe academic and member of the opposition Zimbabwe Unity Movement (ZUM) in the 1990 UC elections.9 A major feature of post-independence LG politics is the escalation of voter apathy in LG elections[10], particularly in low-density areas. This contrasts sharply with cut-throat competition in high-density areas which have witnessed full-scale election campaigns since independence.

Rural Council Reforms

There was little change to the nature and functions of RCs between 1980 and 1987 apart from the choice given to former APAs to either remain as DCs or to become RCs. All SSCFs elected to become RCs, which was a politically sound decision since RCs have as much autonomy as UCs. Developmentally, or economically, however, the decision was detrimental to the SSCFs because they deprived themselves of CG grants which the ZG was providing to DCs in line with its rural development strategy (Helmsing, 1990:91). Consequently, both social services and infrastructural facilities in SSCFs have tended to lag well behind those available in DC areas. One of the several SALA reports notes: "Probably, from the financial point of view, they [RCs] are in an even worse situation than District Councils" (1990:2).

For RCs that are based in LSCFs, however, there has been little change other than that they have attempted to improve on their education, health and welfare facilities taking advantage of CG's grants which cover these areas (Helmsing, 1990:101). The fact that the Lancaster House Constitution (LHC) severely restricted the ZG's land acquisition and land redistribution activities, and to the extent that the colonial LG system was closely linked to the racial division of land, the ZG perceived that changes to the LG system in Zimbabwe's rural areas could only be realistically effected after 1990, i.e. after the mandatory period through which the LHC provisions would have to be observed.

The passing of the Rural Districts Councils (RDCs) Act in 1988 largely laid the groundwork for the amalgamation of DCs and RCs after 1990. This was complemented by the passing of the Land Acquisition Act (LAA 1992) which basically repealed the undesirable restrictions on the ZG's compulsory acquisition of LSCF land for the resettlement of landless Africans. Although the process of amalgamation is in progress at the time of writing, it is possible to make a few initial comments on the implications of the process, and to highlight some of the likely problems and/or consequences of the democratization and unification of the rural LG system in terms of the present study on decentralization. These comments can best be appreciated after a discussion of the pre-amalgamation DCs to which the study will now turn.

District Council Reforms

It has been noted that successive colonial regimes had designed a dual LG system in the rural areas of Zimbabwe with the objective of facilitating "separate development" of the two main race groups. It has also been stated that colonial regimes tried to make use of local authorities in African areas for the purpose of implementing some of their difficult policies which were resisted by the majority African people. A major consequence of these developments was the negative perception that Africans had developed towards LG by the time that independence was attained. The new ZG, therefore, had to propagate the concept of LG to rural-based Africans, highlighting its benefits and dispelling some of the misconceptions that had been generated as a result of the oppressive and discriminatory nature of the colonial LG systems. As noted earlier, LGPOs were the major agents for this purpose.

Some of the post-colonial reforms to DCs have already been covered in an earlier section of this study. The amendment of the District Councils Act (Chapter 231) resulted, *inter alia*, in the creation of larger but fewer DCs which were presumed to be more viable in terms of their capability to marshal local resources and provide efficient and effective goods and services to their citizens. Traditional leaders, who had largely been discredited as agents of LG during the colonial era, were divested of most of their powers which were transferred to democratically elected DCs. For example, the powers to allocate land and to try civil cases among their people were transferred to DCs and to community courts respectively (Mutizwa-Mangiza, 1990:5).

The most significant changes of the post-independence LG system in Zimbabwe's communal areas (CAs) came about as a result of the 1984 and 1985 Prime Minister's Directives (PMD) on decentralization and development. Briefly, these directives, and several pieces of legislation, resulted in the creation of new grassroots structures, the VIDCOs and WADCOs, as noted earlier, and the creation of the Provincial Governors' position, the District Development Committee (DDC), the Provincial Council (PC), and the Provincial Development Committee (PDC), as shown in Figure 1. They, therefore, resulted in the democratization of the LG system in the CAs, which process was consistent with the ruling party's articulated ideology of the liberation struggle period.

Several studies have been undertaken covering some of the major features of the post-colonial LG reforms in Zimbabwe[11]. Only brief comments will be made in this section. As stated earlier, decentralization had been implemented by colonial regimes along racial and ethnic lines. Indeed, most of the names of the eight provinces and fifty-five rural districts are largely indicative of the ethnic groups residing in those areas. A few exceptions were names of colonial figures such as Victoria Province and Mt Darwin District. Some of these names have since been changed, but the majority of provincial names - Manicaland, Mashonaland (East, Central and West) and Matabeleland (North and South) - have continued to the present. Although the ethnic factor does not seem to have caused any significant political problems among Africans in Zimbabwe, the continuity of ethnic names and designations does seem a negation of national unity. John Day (1980:87), writing on the situation obtaining in the short-lived Zimbabwe-Rhodesia states:

> ...the ramifications of political development within the African nationalist movement can be explained more convincingly by dissatisfaction with leaders, rivalries for power, and differences of strategy than by tribe.

While this may have largely been the case during the colonial period in Zimbabwe, there is evidence to the effect that some of the rivalries for power have, indeed, been translated into furious ethnic conflicts, most notably the dissident war in the two Matabeleland provinces prior to 1988. Cases can also be cited of national leaders surrounding themselves with 'home-boys' without regard to skills, educational qualifications or the ability to do the job. With reference to the LG system, the continued ethnic divisions cannot simply be brushed aside because they are evident in the operation of some of the LGUs. It is a well known fact that virtually all Provincial Governors (and Provincial Administrators?) are appointed to areas from which they come in ethnic terms. This is certainly by design rather than by coincidence. Perhaps the assumption is that as political appointees, Provincial Governors have to be acceptable to the citizens of the province if they are to effectively represent the CG and the ruling party at that level. Such an assumption, however, only serves to confirm that ethnicity does have a role to play in the LG system in Zimbabwe, an aspect which requires a more detailed investigation than was possible for the present study.

The PMDs resulted in the creation of some 6 000 VIDCOs, 1 000 WADCOs, and fifty-five rural districts in the eight provinces of Zimbabwe. The VIDCOs and WADCOs were intended to provide the grassroots level in rural areas with an opportunity to participate, in a democratic way, in the decision-making processes for development planning and implementation for their areas. This would not only enable them to have a say in the introduction and management of change in their areas, but would also facilitate their acquisition of the relevant skills, knowledge and attitudes for the shouldering of responsibilities for their own development (Cormack, 1992:9).

The democratic element within the election processes for membership to both the VIDCO and the WADCO was, however, limited in that only four of the six members of the VIDCO were directly elected by the villagers. The remaining two were representatives of the women and the youth leagues of the ruling ZANU/PF party. At the WADCO level, two representatives of these two leagues were also appointed or elected by the leagues themselves rather than by the people in general, or by the VIDCOs. The assumption that every villager was a member of the ruling party, or that other parties or minority groups than those of the ruling ZANU/PF should not be expected to partici- pate in the LG system was a clear but deliberate negation of the democratic process outside of the ruling party. Indeed, authorities are largely agreed that the post-independence LG structure in Zimbabwe was deliberately designed along the structure of ZANU/PF (Stoneman and Cliffe, 1989:79; and Brand, 1991:85). Further, as was stated earlier, the LG structure created as a result of the PMDs and related legislation had the primary objective of facilitating the creation of a one-party state in Zimbabwe:

> The leaders of ZANU have had the creation of a single party (state) in their sights since their overwhelming election victory in 1980. What they have disagreed about is how to bring it about, and (possibly) what kind of single-party system - whether de facto one-party rule, or the enactment of a single-party constitution (Stoneman and Cliffe, 1989:87; *their emphasis*).

This was all in line with the articulated ideology of ZANU/PF which was finally abandoned after the collapse of socialism throughout the world. Very few changes were, however, made to the PMDs and the RDC Act (1988) as a consequence of the abandonment of the socialist approach to national development. Indeed, it can safely be argued that the ruling party in Zimba- bwe is still very much determined to create a *de facto* one-party state since prevailing political trends militate against legislation for a *de jure* one-party system. The realization of *intra elite cohesion*, manifest in the 1987 Unity Accord between ZANU/PF and ZAPU/PF, necessarily reduced the forces of opposition to this approach to the self preservation of ZANU/PF. The implications for democracy at the local level, and within the LG system, are likely to be deleterious, indeed.

Further, the VIDCOs and WADCOs were expected to enable the local people to influence development policies pertaining to their specific areas. The people's representatives at these levels were argued to be fully involved in the identification of local needs and resources, and in the formulation of appropriate solutions and methods of implementing development to ensure that optimum benefits would be reaped by their communities (Cormack, 1992:9-10). Studies have already shown that this assumption was, basically, erroneous since, as shall be argued later, there are too many inhibitions that beset both VIDCOs and WADCOs in the execution of these developmental and democratic roles.[12]

Each village is represented at the WADCO level by the chairman and secretary of the VIDCO. Each WADCO, in turn, is represented by its chairman at the RDC level. Six villages constitute a ward, a district can have as many wards as there are groups of six villages to be represented. The fact that traditionally, villages do not always have the same number of people has resulted in villages and wards of various population sizes across the country. This issue is discussed fully by Brand (1991:85-88) who states in part, 'In Mutoko District...the locally estimated populations of the 18 Communal Area wards ranged from 4 748 to 7 021 and the villages from 461 (30 households) to 1 767 (156 households).'

This may seem a minor point but it has implications for democracy, for example in terms of equitable representation of the various wards. In terms of the provision of benefits, this problem was actually found to be a serious one in the Buhera District where this author did research for a separate study.[13] During the 1991/92 drought period, villagers in the Matsveru ward complained that they were receiving far less drought relief food than their counterparts from smaller wards. The number of households in the Matsveru district was nearly three times that of most other adjacent wards. The headman of the area, with the full co-operation of the VIDCO and WADCO leaders, decided to split the ward into three 'separate' units for the purposes of distribution of drought relief. The fact remains, however, that the people of the area are under-represented in the DC, while those in smaller wards were over-represented. Interviews with the councillor who represents Matsveru ward revealed that he did not mind representing such a large ward. He was opposed to a permanent reduction of the number of households under his ward.

As pointed out earlier, the district level is the focus of this study. It is at this level that meaningful decentralization ends, at least, in terms of the legal framework within which post-independence decentralization was carried out.

Both the WADCO and the VIDCO do not have corporate or statutory status exclusive of that derived from the one conferred upon the DC. Once fully constituted, the DC proceeds to elect its own chairman, secretary, treasurer, and other committee members. The DC chairman and one other councillor represent the DC at the Provincial Council (PC) level. The youth and the women of each province are also represented in the PC by one member each. These members are appointed by the President, and the practice to date has been to appoint representatives who are nominated by the ZANU/PF women and youth leagues. There is no evidence to the effect that opposition political parties and other women and youth organizations were ever consulted on the appointments.[14]

As Figure 1 indicates, the Provincial Development Committee (PDC) and the District Development Committee (DDC) constitute part of the deconcentrated authority of the CG at the provincial and district levels respectively. These two structures are dominated by CG officials from the various ministries and agencies, but they also have representatives from both the PC and the DC respectively. The major functions of both the PDC and the DDC are to plan, implement and co-ordinate development activities at their levels. In doing so they are required to work closely with the elective bodies at each level, who are also expected to approve of the plans before they are passed on to the National Planning Agency or Commission for inclusion in the national plans. A number of problems seem to be associated with this arrangement of decision-making at the provincial and district levels in terms of decentralization and democracy. Before briefly discussing some of these problems, however, it is necessary to note a few elements of the Provincial Governor (PG) position, which is also part of decentralization.

Under the colonial LG system, provincial administrative structures were headed by the Provincial Commissioner, who was a senior civil servant within the Ministry of Internal Affairs. The post-independence counterpart is the Provincial Administrator (PA) who has the rank of Under Secretary in the MLGRUD. The PDC, which comprises all provincial heads of the various CG ministries and departments, is chaired by the PA. The 1984/85 PMDs resulted, *inter alia*, in the creation of PGs who are political appointees made by the President. PGs are appointed from among members of Parliament, and they have recently been elevated to ministerial status.

A PG has 'political, consultative, developmental and co-ordinative' functions (Zimbabwe Government, 1984:2). As senior political representatives of the CG at the provincial level, PGs are answerable to the political leadership, i.e. the President and the Cabinet. They have the right of access to all CG agencies and agents, and to all political parties operating at the provincial level. They chair the PCs but may not direct them as to what decisions to make apart from those relating to the conducting of meetings. They are expected to have close working relationships with the PAs and other provincial heads of ministries who, however, do not report directly to them, but are expected to inform them of developments in the province. The primary task of the PGs is, therefore, 'the co-ordinated development of their respective provinces' (Zimbabwe Government, 1984:2).

The operations of the PGs' offices are financed through the MLGRUD. This ministry also provides the personnel and other facilities needed by the PGs. Because they are representatives of the CG and not those of the provincial citizens, PGs do not constitute what may be regarded as democratic leadership at the provincial level. The PCs which they chair do not consist of directly elected representatives of the people in the province. In fact, most of the members of the PC have more allegiance to their districts, or DCs and UCs than to the PC. The PC can, therefore, not be argued to be an expression of the democratic will of the provincial citizens.

Further, because it lacks, almost completely, any meaningful resource base, the PC can only be argued to have very limited devolved authority. Indeed, the DC has more devolved authority than the PC in substantive terms. It is the view of this study that the creation of the post of PG was superfluous and unnecessarily costly to the Zimbabwean tax-payer. Apart from the performance of a few ceremonial functions, which can easily be performed by city mayors and DC chairmen, the creation of the PG is of no redeeming value to the LG system at the sub-national level in Zimbabwe. This was indisputably demonstrated during the 1991/92 drought season when the President appointed Provincial 'Resident Ministers' to oversee the distribution of drought relief food in the provinces. Any top level government official who cannot be relied upon to effectively supervise the distribution of relief food to starving peasants is, certainly, not capable of enhancing the effectiveness and efficiency of a LG system at regional and sub-regional levels. This study further contents that the creation of PGs was consistent with the creation of a single-party political system in Zimbabwe. Apart from facilitating the provision of jobs to devout, but largely lacklustre, ruling party adherents, the appointment of PGs served to increase ZANU/PF's political influence at the provincial and district levels, albeit, in a top-down way.

Observations on DCs Since 1980

On the positive side, it must be acknowledged that the notion of democratizing the LG system in post-independence Zimbabwe was a virtuous one since it meant that the grassroots could, for the first time, actively participate in the affairs of their local areas. The removal of the racial factor from the LG system was also commendable since it enabled the masses to realize that their development was now their own responsibility, and that there no longer was an easily (or racially) identifiable impediment to their self-determination. Indeed, whereas under the colonial LG system the DCs fell under the Ministry of Internal Affairs while the RCs and UCs were under the Ministry of Local Government and Housing, after 1980, all local authorities became the charge of the MLGRUD. Further, the reduction of the powers of traditional leaders, though initially implemented as a form of retribution for their past collusion with the colonialists, was indicative of a post-independence regime legitimately interested in creating a viable, democratic LG system in Zimbabwe. As pointed out earlier, the fact that some of the traditional powers are now being reinstated is largely a function of the political decay, departicipation and depoliticization, generally, characteristic of neo-colonial polities.

The creation of grassroots organizations - the VIDCO and the WADCO - facilitated democratic decision-making which NGOs have been able to make good use of (Mutizwa-Mangiza, 1990:7). Indeed, some VIDCOs and WADCOs are now more actively involved in NGO sponsored development activities than they are in government sponsored ones. Although there is evidence to the effect that some VIDCOs are not operating as effectively as they were initially intended to (Brand, 1991:87), their existence provides certain administrative benefits to deconcentrated CG structures:

> They have replaced the colonial headman's and post-independence party assemblies as the key vehicle for conveying information to the populace regarding government programmes and intentions. They can be used as a sounding-board and forum for consultation by line administrators and extension staff. They can be given the responsibility of marshalling people and assisting in the implementation of land use plans or infrastructure projects. They can also act as a buffer between communities and the administration and outside agencies, by insisting that all demands or proposals from below, or external initiatives, be channelled through, and be approved by the VIDCO/WADCOs (and Rural District Council where appropriate). This establishes a gate-keeping function which is not controlled by the community alone, but involves other outside institutions which can bring considerable pressures to bear on decisions and action (Brand, 1991:92).

Further, these grassroots organizations are useful for educating the masses and providing them with experience in decision-making, development and democratic governance. Thus by expediting community participation in grassroots development, and constituting crucial contact points for external change agents, VIDCOs and WADCOs can be argued to be making a positive contribution to democratic governance at the grassroots level. The impact of their contribution, and, therefore, that of decentralization, on the evolution of a democratic system of governance in Zimbabwe, however, is the subject of the present study. The study, according to its findings, contends that the ideal situation painted above does not, in fact, exist in reality. There are also some negative aspects of the post-colonial decentralization processes and decentralized institutions which have a bearing on democracy and development in Zimbabwe.

On the negative side of the decentralization process in Zimbabwe since 1980, it is fair to argue that, to a considerable extent, the principal objective of the PMDs and their related pieces of legislation was to facilitate the co-optation and mobilization of the grassroots to support and participate in centrally initiated, financed and controlled development programmes (Brand, 1991:80). This is not necessarily an objective inimical to participatory development and democracy. The fact that it projects a false impression of the empowerment of the grassroots, however, negates their democratic participation in the long run.

As shall be shown later, the lack of adequate authority for local resource raising at the district and lower levels has meant that LG institutions at these levels have remained dependent on CG for their survival. CG has also, basically, dictated the *modus operandi* of these institutions. There has been little room for innovation and initiative for these decentralized bodies and the result has tended to be a slow process of ossification. Both the VIDCOs and the WADCOs do not have any authority to raise local resources among their citizens. Neither do they receive any funds from CG. The development proposals they submit to the DC and higher bodies largely remain on paper. This frustrates them and reduces their penchant for participation in meaningful decision-making and democratic governance.

DCs, because they receive the bulk of their resources from CG (Helmsing, 1991:129; Wekwete, 1988:23; MLGRUD/SALA, 1990:8).[15] tend to be constrained in the taking of local initiative and democratic decision-making. It has already been indicated that DDCs, i.e. deconcentrated bodies, do most of the actual development planning at the district level, while DCs simply approve the district plans before they are forwarded to the PC/PDCs. This situation will, however, be slightly rectified when the RDC Act (1988) is fully implemented.[16] The fact, nevertheless, remains that democratically elected representatives of the people do not have the opportunity of making development decisions based on the wishes of the people they represent.

In devising the post-independence LG system at the district level, the ZG has largely maintained the inherited prefectoral system (Mutizwa-Mangiza, 1990:8) which will be significantly changed when the DCs are amalgamated with the RCs to create RDCs. But even then, the 'mixed authority' approach to LG will be in evidence since the RDDC will still be performing the critical aspect of development planning and, therefore, resource allocation. Generally, most post-independence LG reforms fail to address the problem of socio-economic differentiation among the peasants in Zimbabwe's CAs (Brand, 1991:83). Government's persuasion of the grassroots to elect into DCs people who can understand government policies and programmes only serves to exacerbate this problem. The LG reforms are likely to be of benefit, mainly to the rural rich, the majority of whom also benefited from the colonial LG system. Indeed, the resurgence of the powers of traditional leaders attests to this tentative conclusion. Finally, the need to renovate the whole LG system in the light of the abandonment of the socialist ideology and the authoritarian one-party system is a prerequisite for the evolution of a democratic LG system in Zimbabwe.

4
Post-Independence Decentralisation and Development

Most documents relating to the post-independence LG system in Zimbabwe are emphatic that the primary role of decentralisation is the facilitation of development at the local level, and with the participation of the people. There seems to be an assumption that the democratisation of the LG system would necessarily lead to beneficiary participation in the development process and self-reliance. The findings of this study indicate that there are conflicting views on the success that decentralisation has achieved in bringing about both development and democracy to the local level. This section will focus on the impact of decentralisation on the development process in Zimbabwe. The views of the various categories of respondents will be discussed separately.

Popular Participation in Development: The Official View
The majority of government and local authority officials interviewed for this study were of the opinion that, generally, decentralisation has resulted in increased public participation in policy formulation and development, at least, relative to the situation obtaining prior to the attainment of national independence. They, however, conceded that the policy formulation process is largely top-down in nature in Zimbabwe, and the people's participation in the process has largely been in reaction to policy proposals from the top. There has been little of policy initiatives from the people themselves. The same situation seems to have obtained with regard to development initiatives. The CG, through its deconcentrated (field) agents, makes the majority of the decisions of what to include in local development plans, and what resources should be made available for the implementation of these projects.

Further, there was ample evidence to indicate that appointed officials exercise more authority than elected people's representatives at the district and provincial levels of the LG structure. Government officials justified this undemocratic situation by arguing that they are the ones who have information on what resources the CG will make available for the implementation of development programmes and projects, so they should make the critical decisions regarding these programmes and projects if they are to be funded. They further alleged that the majority of the elected representatives of the people do not have appropriate planning and budgeting skills to enable them to participate effectively in these processes.

Officials of the District Councils Association, however, contended that the people's participation in development is largely restricted to the implementation of government initiated development programmes and projects rather than to the formulation, design and implementation of the people's own projects. As a result, according to these officials, there have been cases of public resistance to participate in some of the government initiated programmes and projects, except under severe hardships such as drought. For example, in Chipinge and parts of Matabeleland South, some people have complained that the four dollars (about US$0,60) per day they were paid by the CG after participating in the 'Food-for-Work' programme was grossly inadequate for their needs, or for the amount of work they did.[17]

In Gwanda, an administrative officer in the District Administration office indicated that although public participation in local development increased significantly soon after the implementation of the PMDs, there has recently been a marked decrease in the level of the people's participation, which he attributed to apathy among the people. In Bikita, a similarly placed officer asserted that people basically participate in government initiated development programmes on the insistence of technocrats and public servants. The reason for this, he argued, is that most people are afraid to refuse to participate in these programmes because of the possible repercussions from both the ZG and the ruling party, ZANU/PF.[18] It is possible that, with increased political liberalism in Zimbabwe, the level of beneficiary participation in government initiated development programmes might decrease even further.

The majority of CG and LGU appointed officials claimed that elected people's representatives make the critical decisions at both the district and provincial levels of the LG structure in Zimbabwe. Field research findings, however, indicate that the critical decisions regarding resource allocation, project identification, formulation and programme planning are all the preserve of appointed officials of the CG at both these levels. The Provincial Administrator for Matabeleland South, for example, accepted that elected people's representatives merely approve what will already have been decided upon by government appointees at both levels. In approving these decisions, elected officials are not expected to make any significant changes to the DDC or PDC decisions, although they may ask the civil servants to consider making some adjustments to some of their proposals. The Gutu District Administrator justified this situation by claiming that people do not know what they want; it is therefore, incumbent upon the administrators to make the critical decisions which will further the development of their local areas. He further argued that the majority of the people's representatives are still at the learning stage of their responsibilities, and someone has to make the decisions. The truth is that the LG system as presently constituted in Zimbabwe does not lend itself to the making of any meaningful decisions by local representatives of the people. Elected representatives tend to learn much faster if they make the critical decisions themselves, even if they may make mistakes at first. There is no better way of learning. It is difficult, for example, to demonstrate that elected representatives are learning how to plan and budget by simply considering the submissions of public servants at the Joint Meetings of the DDC and DC, or of the PDC and the PC.

Obviously, the major reason why elected representatives at both the district and provincial levels do not have the authority to make the critical decisions is that they lack the resources needed for the development of their own areas. As noted earlier, DCs receive more than 90% while PCs receive 100% of their funding from the ZG throughout the MLGRUD. Confirming this, one respondent stated:

> Councillors may make decisions but the DC has no power. For example, DC minutes are sent to the Provincial Administrator. If the decisions are perceived to be in conflict with central government's position or policies, the Provincial Administrator can amend them in consultation with central government. Consequently, the DCs end up receiving directives from central government.[19]

Another factor which militates against meaningful decision-making by the local people's representatives is the fact that the CG has persistently refused to decentralise the national budget. Thus instead of providing provinces and districts with resources which they then can decide how to allocate among proposed development activities, the ZG requires that all proposals be submitted to it for approval and inclusion in the national budget and national development plans. The result is that the majority of the proposals from the villages, wards and districts are excluded from the national budget, or from the plans since there will not be adequate resources for their implementation. DCs and PCs, in turn, discover that their planning and budgeting efforts result in no meaningful returns in terms of funded development activities, and see no point in further participation in these processes.

Effect of Decentralisation on Government Operations
When decentralisation is carried out for the purpose of facilitating public participation in local development and governance it also tends to be used by

CG 'to soften resistance to the profound social changes which development entails' (Smith, 1985:187). CG plans, policies and programmes for change and development are channelled through decentralised institutions which are, in many cases, expected to adopt them as their own initiatives. This will not only enable CG to implement unpopular policies and programmes, but will also garner support for these policies and programmes from local communities:

> Decentralisation can secure commitment to developments needing a change of attitudes. National development may produce social disorganisation and political instability . . . Local government can ease the process of change by providing local leadership to win support for change by involvement. Conflict can be turned in constructive directions. Decentralisation is seen as a means of 'penetrating' rural areas (Smith, 1985:187).

But there is also a way in which decentralisation can be used by local communities to resist the imposition and implementation of unacceptable government and local government plans, policies and programmes. LG institutions at the grassroots level, once created, tend to be viewed by the people as multi-purpose institutions which they can make use for a variety of objectives. This section will discuss appointed officials' views on the way in which decentralisation has facilitated people's resistance to unacceptable policies, increased scrutiny of government operations by the people, and enabled CG to implement unpopular plans, policies and programmes.

It was noted earlier that the LG structures which resulted from the PMDs and related legislation was deliberately patterned along the ZANU/PF party structure of the liberation struggle period. Since independence, the ruling party has been noted for ruthlessly dealing with all kinds of opposition to the party (or government) line. Post-independence decentralisation has only been used by local communities to resist unacceptable government policies and programmes to a very limited extent. Fear of the wrath of the ruling party has largely been the major factor militating against effective use of LG structures for the purposes of resisting unacceptable government decisions.

A Bikita 'Assistant' District Administrator[20] stated that local people have largely not resisted unacceptable government policies for fear of repercussions from both the party and CG. Public scrutiny of government operations is also inhibited by the same fear among the people. The officer further indicated that local people who are opposed to certain government policies tend to express their opposition through other organisations which are not part of the LG system. Consequently, decentralisation has enabled the ZG to enforce some unpopular policies and programmes, including certain local authority by-laws which have their origins in the colonial era. The officer gave examples of dog tax, cart license fees and development levy.

The District Administrator of Chivi confirmed that people in his area have also attempted to resist the payment of these fees and levies, which they regard as oppressive, but decentralisation facilitated their compliance with the law. The Chivi District Administrator agreed that decentralisation is a powerful tool in the hands of CG in that it not only facilitates the people's compliance with unacceptable government policies, but also enables CG to mobilise support for its unpopular policies and programmes at the local village and ward level. Some of these CG initiated policies and programmes are hardly discussed by members of the DC. Their choice in either supporting or rejecting these policies is therefore rather limited.

Contrary to this view, an officer with the Midlands Public Administrator's office claimed that public scrutiny of government operations has increased as a result of decentralisation. She indicated that ordinary citizens now question public servants when projects are not completed on time, or not implemented in accordance with council decisions. The Joint Meetings of the RDC and the DDC and those of the PC and the PDC have been used for this purpose in the Midlands Province. This was echoed by the Gokwe DA who cited the example of the criticism levelled at his officers regarding the way drought relief was distributed in the area. The Gokwe people also complained when the War Veterans did not distribute game meat after shooting wild animals in their areas.[21]

Further, in Manicaland, several other examples of how citizens made use of decentralisation to resist unpopular government policies were provided by the Provincial Administrator who cited the Makoni people's opposition to the construction of the Osborne dam. The dam, currently under construction, will displace hundreds of families when full. Although the people made use of their local representatives to express their opposition to the project, it was the LG grassroots institutions which eventually managed to persuade the people to allow CG to proceed with the project. The DC argued that the dam was to be of long-term benefit to the people of the area. In Maungwe District, according to the Senior Executive Officer of the DC, the ESAP and the resettlement programme have been criticised by the people through LG structures. In both these cases, as in many others, CG has largely ignored the voices of the people and proceeded to implement its policies. In Maungwe District, for example, CG made good use of decentralised structures to enforce the unpopular gully reclamation policy. In some areas, the policy of villagisation has been enforced through VIDCOs and WADCOs despite the citizens' opposition to the programme. The Mahere village citizens have to date refused to comply with CG's wishes to implement the same policy, but officials of both the district and the council administration agree that the people will eventually have to accept the programme because it is linked to the provision of such basic essentials as reticulated water, electricity and properly managed grazing areas for their livestock. In the Chipinge District, the DC was instrumental in articulating the people's opposition to the citing of Checheche Microwave Tower at a traditionally sacred place. The DC, however, persuaded the local people to allow the erection of the tower after they had been allowed to perform certain traditional rituals. Citizens interviewed in the area indicated that they are still very unhappy about the defilement of their sacred locale.

It would appear that there are some areas in which the people have taken some advantage of decentralisation to resist government policies and programmes which they perceive as unacceptable to them. There are also areas in which the government has not met this kind of resistance from the local people. This study found out that most opposition to CG policies and programmes comes from Manicaland and Matabeleland South Provinces, while there is very little or no opposition at all from most of Masvingo, and the Mashonaland Provinces. Resistance to government policies and programmes seems to have emanated from provinces which have had a long history of supporting opposition parties, while provinces which have traditionally been the ruling party's strongholds have tended to comply with whatever the ZG has sought to implement at the local level. For its part, the CG has largely made use of LGUs as a device for the furtherance of its own objectives regarding change and development in Zimbabwe's CAs. In the final analysis, it becomes evident that decentralisation in Zimbabwe since 1984 has largely tended to promote the interests of CG at the expense of those of local communities.

Citizens' Views on District Councils and Development

One of the major objectives of decentralisation is the promotion of social and economic development at the local level (Laleye and Olowu). LG institutions such as provincial and district councils are expected to facilitate local social and economic development through the provision of goods and services which will result in the improvement of the living standards of the local people. The goods and services provided should, ideally, be consonant with the demands and needs of the people. The extent to which decentralisation enhances meaningful development at the sub-national level determines its acceptance and that of the resultant institutions. Smith (1985:185) argues that, in most Third World countries, the developmental burden which has been placed upon decentralisation has been too great for it to manage:

> ... decentralisation has been seen as particularly relevant to meeting the needs of the poor. It is argued that if development is to mean the eradication of poverty, inequality and material deprivation it must engage the involvement and mobilisation of the poor (Smith, 1985:186).

The same sentiments were echoed by the President of Zimbabwe while addressing an inauguration congress of the Association of District Councils. He pointed out that DCs, because they are located close to the people, are better able to determine "both the form and direction of development" than central government institutions.[22] This section of the study focuses on the views of ordinary citizens on the role of DCs in the development process. Respondents were, in the main, asked specific questions, as listed in Table 1, in relation to their DC and the local DA's office. Although a few individual citizens were interviewed for this section, the majority of respondents were in groups of between five and ten people.

Development and Democracy in Zimbabwe

Table 1
Focus Groups' Views on the Developmental Role of DCs

	CHIPINGE		MAUNGWE		CHIVI		GUTU		GWANDA		GOKWE		KADOMA	
	Y	N	Y	N	Y	N	Y	N	Y	N	Y	N	Y	N
- Does DC facilitate development?	X		X				X		X		X			X
- Are you satisfied with DC's work?	X			X			X		X		X			X
- Are you satisfied with DA's work?	X				X			X		X		X		X
- DA officers better than pre-1980?	X		X			X		X		X		X		X
- Received any benefits from DC?	X		X				X		X		X			X
- Received any benefits from DA's?		X	X		X			X		X		X		X
- Is DC good system for local affairs?	X			X			X		X		X		X	
- Does DC really serve your interests?		X	X				X		X		X			X

The findings of this study reveal that there are significantly conflicting views among people regarding the utility and relevance of decentralisation or local government institutions to local development. It would appear though, that most of the respondents in a given area were agreed on the major aspects of their DC even where two or three Focus Groups were interviewed. A major contributor to the type of responses obtained was the level of success of the DC in meeting the developmental needs of the local people. Where the DC has largely been unable to either facilitate CG intervention in local problems or obtain NGO or other donor assistance for developmental purposes, the citizens have tended to view the DC in a negative light. The reverse seems to have been true for successful DCs in the areas under study.

Responses to the eight items listed in Table 1 indicated that in four of the seven districts, respondents were of the view that their DCs were useful in facilitating local development. They agreed that their DCs served their interests in mobilising people and resources for social and economic development. In Maungwe, the three focus groups were not agreed on the final item in Table 1. Two of the groups felt that although their DC represented their interests, it was not successful in bringing about meaningful development to their area. Four districts were not satisfied with the work of their DC but five out of the seven districts indicated that they were satisfied with the work of the DA's office. It must, however, be borne in mind that the DA's offices throughout Zimbabwe were particularly active during the period of this study because of the devastating drought of 1991/92.

Almost all the focus groups agreed that decentralisation which results in the creation of local institutions for participatory development constituted a good system of local government. The one exception was Kadoma where the respondents indicated that they had not received any benefits from their DC in any form. All the three focus groups in this district concurred on virtually every item on the questionnaire regarding the failure of both their DC and that of the DA's office in meeting their developmental needs. Finally, in only two districts, Chipinge and Kadoma, were district administration officers perceived not to perform better than colonial administrators. For the most part and in both districts, the major reasons were political rather than developmental in nature. For example, in Chipinge respondents were unanimous that because their district was noted for supporting an opposition party they were being punished by CG through the appointment of district officers who had a "bad attitude" towards the local people, and who were of low calibre. They also charged that their locally elected councillors were of low calibre, and unskilled in representing their interests. Therefore, the DC ends up implementing only those decisions that are of interest to the CG or to the councillors. It may be useful to examine closely some of the positive and negative responses made by the various focus groups in order to identify selected aspects of decentralisation that the respondents highlighted.

Respondents were largely agreed that, as presently constituted, DCs provided a link between the people and the government. Apart from facilitating the flow of information from the top to the people, the DCs also provided a forum through which objections to unacceptable CG policies and programmes could be articulated. DCs were noted for providing local employment opportunities to a few local people in normal times, and to many more people through the food-for-work programmes. In most areas, although this programme was funded by the ZG it was largely managed by the DCs with the assistance of the local DA's office. In some districts, respondents indicated that they have benefited from the clinics, schools, roads, dams and other infrastructural activities undertaken by their DCs.

A focus group of five people in Gwanda was strongly supportive of the work of their DC which they praised for representing them effectively with regard to unpopular CG policies and programmes. They were also able to list a number of benefits which they had received as a result of the work of their DC. It did appear though, that the majority of the benefits were obtained from NGOs which approached the DC, and those which sought the approval of their proposed projects through VIDCOs and WADCOs. For some reason, the local people were of the view that NGOs were able to operate effectively in their areas because they were authorised or invited by their local DC. While this may be the case in some districts, it certainly was not true for all the districts under study.

Positive responses were also indicated regarding the DA's office in some of the seven districts. In Gwanda, for example, all three focus groups agreed that the DA's office had been positively instrumental in ensuring that the local people would, not only be able to receive adequate levels of drought relief through the food-for-work programme, but could also preserve their livestock by grazing them in the resettlement areas without charge or harassment.In both Gutu and Chivi of the Masvingo Provinces, respondents indicated that they had benefited from the work of the district administration which they argued to be much better than the colonial ones. They pointed out that CG benefits to peasant farmers were channelled through the DA's office and not through their DCs which they considered to be very inefficient. In the Gokwe District, respondents pointed out that the fact that they are consulted before any new projects are undertaken by the DA's office makes the present district administration a lot better than the colonial administration. In almost all the districts that had positive comments about their district administrators, focus groups had indicated that they were not satisfied with the performance levels of their DCs. This comparison is crucial to this study since it seems to imply that the current LG system in Zimbabwe leans more towards local administration than local government.

Negative comments on the nature of DCs were largely based on the level of performance of these bodies *vis-a-vis* the expectations, demands and needs of the respective citizens. Very few focus groups agreed that DCs may be unable to perform to their expectations because of limited financial and other resources. On the contrary, most focus groups were of the opinion that councillors were more interested in spending the citizens' money than in undertaking meaningful development activities in their areas. This indicated that in many areas, councillors had not adequately educated the people they represent on the financial situation obtaining in DCs.

Thus, while agreeing that decentralisation was the correct approach in facilitating local development, the focus groups interviewed in Chipinge asserted that their DC was doing very little to develop the area. They further claimed that NGOs do most of the developmental work in the Chipinge area and therefore serve the interests of the people. One focus group alleged that there was too much favouritism in the operations of the DC which left most of the needy people stranded for basic needs and benefits which others in the same district would be receiving. They specifically mentioned that the distribution of development projects is always skewed in favour of the administrators' favoured areas but declined to name the areas. Both district administration and DC officials denied these allegations. They further alleged that DCs do not serve the interests of the people but come up with their own policies and programmes which serve their own interests, and which are contrary to the wishes of the people.

A focus group in the Maungwe District alleged that there was too much bureaucracy in their DC, which caused it to fail to respond to the needs of the people, and which resulted in serious delays in the implementation of development projects. One of the focus groups in this district was adamant that without the support and co-operation of traditional leaders, DCs would not be successful in bringing about meaningful development in the rural areas of Zimbabwe. At least four other focus groups in the districts under study held similar views on the role of traditional leaders in local government institutions.

Perhaps the most vocal focus groups against a DC were those interviewed in the Chivi District. The first group of five people was so vehemently opposed to the DC that they stated categorically that the DC should be abolished, or absorbed by the DA's office, or that the DA should run the DC directly to make it more efficient. They alleged that their DC does 'nothing but squander our money,' they do not solve any of the problems that are faced by the local people. They further claimed that they had not received any benefits from their DC but had been greatly assisted by the local DA's office, and by NGOs and other donor agencies. The same views were expressed by two other focus groups in the same district, one of which further alleged that their DC was only interested in imposing all manner of levies, fees and charges but without undertaking any meaningful development activities in the area. In the Gokwe District, focus groups also expressed dissatisfaction with their DC which they accused of not providing them with any benefits

In almost all of the districts where negative comments were expressed against the DC, the respondents indicated that they were much happier with the operations of the DA's office than with those of their DC. This was the case even in districts where the distribution of drought relief food was done by the DC and not by the DA's office. Further, in all these districts, focus groups located in different wards tended to hold very similar views about their DC. It is the strong assumption of this study that the nature of the structure of the

LG system in Zimbabwe results in the vilification of the DC as an inefficient and ineffective LG structure because of institutional constraints beyond its capability to ameliorate. The limited resource base is one such constraint which could possibly be alleviated by CG through the decentralisation of the national budget as shall be argued later. But there were also negative comments made regarding the operations of the district administration offices in some of the areas under study.

In Chipinge, for example, two focus groups alleged that district administrators are hardly ever seen outside their offices. They were therefore accused of being unable to accurately determine the developmental needs of the area under their administrative jurisdiction. They were accused of lacking respect for the local people, in which case their behaviour was regarded as basically similar to that of the colonial administrators. Indeed, in one highly emotional focus group in the Chipinge District, respondents, in a focus group of ten people, insisted that Ian Smith's district[23] administrators were much better behaved than the post-independence administrators in the area.

They further argued that during the colonial period, colonial administrators used to implement what they would have promised the people: 'But now the promises are broken as soon as the meeting ends.' Expressing virtually the same sentiments, a focus group of seven citizens in a different ward of the same district indicated that they had no confidence in their district administrators, whom they suspected of practising favouritism in the distribution of CG approved development projects. In the Gwanda District, two focus groups were of the opinion that although their DA was 'a good person' he did not visit them in their villages, and was therefore unaware of the conditions under which they lived, nor could he understand their articulated developmental needs.

In Chivi District, respondents alleged that some of them were harsh with people and very difficult to approach. Although the majority of them were much better behaved than colonial administrators, they were still hampered by bureaucratic considerations in their operations. They are therefore also inflicted with the problem of failure to fulfil promises to the people. In one of the focus groups in the Midlands Province respondents accused the DA of calling them 'council people' and 'not government people.' Thus whenever the people approached the DA with their problems he would ask them to approach their DC since he claimed that he had nothing to do with them.

Members of a focus group of seven people in the Mashonaland district alleged that their DA was disinterested in the development of their local area because he came from another district; he was not born in their area. They, in fact, alleged that their DA was actively involved in the development of

Zvimba District, his home area, while doing very little to develop the district in which he was DA.

The major fault that respondents seemed to point out with regard to the district administration was the 'excuse' of lack of finances to implement development projects. Citizens were not convinced that CG was usually slow in releasing funds for local development even when specific projects had been approved and included in the national development plans. This, once again, is a problem brought about by the centralisation of the national budget, and the dependence of local administration on centrally generated and allocated resources.

5
The Political Dimension of Decentralisation: The Official View

The previous section has discussed some of the developmental expectations of citizens in various parts of Zimbabwe in relation to the LG system in general, and the DCs in particular. It has been noted that the DCs' failure to effectively respond to local demands and needs for the improvement of living standards and the provision of essential services has attracted, possibly, the most critical responses from the grassroots in the seven districts under study. The reason for this is that, generally, citizens expect LG institutions at the local level to provide alternative mechanisms for dealing with and solving local problems. LG is, therefore, viewed as community governance (Green *et al*, 1991:11), and as facilitating community participation, not only in local social and economic development, but also in local 'self-governance.' As pointed out throughout the previous section, the major problem in the Zimbabwe LG system seems to be the dominating role that the CG plays in virtually all aspects of local development. There is evidence that the same situation obtains with regard to the local governance, or the political aspects of LG and decentralisation in Zimbabwe.

One of the objectives of decentralisation is the creation of LG institutions which can play a significant role in the 'development of political responsibility' among the local level citizens:

> As formal institutions of government, they can serve as training grounds for future national leaders. Once involved in activities in their own areas, these leaders become spokesmen for the nation to the people of their own regions. Adequate local government institutions can be the bedrock on which the nation is built (Gorvine, 1965:229).

The political dimension of decentralisation requires that a study of DCs as representative political institutions be undertaken in order to determine the impact of decentralisation on the process of democratic local or community governance. As stated in an earlier section of this study, DCs constitute the lowest level of legally devolved political power in Zimbabwe. How democratic are they in both character and in terms of their operations? Do they, in fact, foster meaningful citizen participation in local decision-making along democratic lines, or are they mere extensions of CG to the local level? Do members of DCs learn much about political responsibility, democracy, liberty and other elements of a just and equal opportunity oriented society? Finally, to what extent do they facilitate the democratisation of bureaucracy in Zimbabwe? This study does not claim to have answers to all these questions. The views of respondents to a number of items on a structured questionnaire will, it is hoped, assist in furnishing some of the answers to these questions. For systematic discussion of the findings, the responses are once again divided into two categories: viz official views and citizens' views.

Impact of Decentralisation on State, Politics and Society - The Official view

The study was able to establish that there are many conflicting views among both elected and appointed officials of decentralised structures in Zimbabwe. The dominant trend, however, seems to be that officials are well aware that as currently structured, the LG system in Zimbabwe leaves a lot to be desired in terms of facilitating democratic governance of local areas. The majority of those interviewed were of the opinion that decentralisation as per the PMDs and related legislation has not resulted in either meaningful distribution of political and administrative power, or the empowerment of sub-national and sub-regional LG institutions for effective decision-making. Indeed, one appointed official insisted that decentralisation has not yet been implemented in Zimbabwe, even though the relevant structures have been set up.[24] A closer examination of some of the responses is undertaken below.

Strong State - Weak Society

Migdal (1988:32) contends that the real politics of Third World countries over the years has been manifest in the state's desire for predominance, the arrangements that are made between the state and other actors in the environment, and the pursuit of the best deal by these actors. The struggles for the best deal, and therefore for predominance, Migdal argues, has taken place away from the capital cities of most of these countries. The various actors fight one another over 'social control,' which Migdal claims, is the *currency* which can be measured or assessed through an examination of three key factors - *compliance, participation* and *legitimation*.

A comprehensive discussion of these factors and their relation to the notion of 'strong state - weak society' is beyond the scope of this present study. Suffice it to note that the state's capability to demand compliance rests, primarily, on its capacity to control various kinds of resources and services, for which it has to compete with other organisations in the environment, including the people's own groups. Secondly, as Migdal (1988:32) aptly states: 'Participation denotes repeated voluntary use of and action in state-run or state-authorised institutions.' The participation of personnel with specialised skills coupled with the citizens' participation in these institutions strengthens the state. Finally, noting that legitimation is the 'most potent factor' which accounts for the strength of the state, Migdal (1988:33) writes:

> It is an acceptance, even approbation, of the state's rules of the game, its social control, as true and right . . . legitimacy includes the acceptance of the state's symbolic configuration within which the rewards and sanctions are packaged. It indicates people's approval of the state's desired social order through their acceptance of the state's myths.

This study largely focused on legitimation and participation in order to determine the strength of the Zimbabwe state *vis-a-vis* that of society. Nevertheless, the element of compliance is also implied in such aspects of the study as the people's resistance to unpopular government policies and programmes, and the general apathy pervading the operations of many LGUs in the districts under study. It is the contention of this study that, given the foregoing discussion, decentralisation has been a major instrument for social control, which the state has made use of to its advantage, and which has resulted in the weakening of society and its organisations.

Almost all the respondents agreed that decentralisation in Zimbabwe has resulted in a very strong state.[25] The Senior Executive Officer (SEO) of Chipinge District Council, for example, argued that currently, the decentralisation system in Zimbabwe is deficient in that it is more of a (ruling)party structure than a national LG system. Thus, while the current structure strengthens the ruling party, it actually weakens the state and those parts of society that are not part of the ruling party. This has had serious implications for democracy in Zimbabwe, as shall be shown later. The same sentiments were echoed by a number of other DC and district administration officials who further indicated that the current structure of decentralisation in Zimbabwe has largely facilitated CG penetration of the periphery for purposes of control and manipulation of the local people. Consequently, local citizens have realised that their DCs have no capacity for meaningfully representing them, or facilitating the meeting of their developmental needs. Some have since withdrawn from active participation in DC initiated development ventures; they have lost confidence in the LGUs as agents for appropriate local development and governance. In short, this has resulted in the weakening of society as a whole.

Respondents were largely agreed that decentralisation in Zimbabwe effectively links the state and the society, but in an asymmetric fashion which ensures that the former benefits from the relationship at the expense of the latter. One of the major reasons for the weakening of society under decentralisation in Zimbabwe is the partial nature of the process. Officials were largely agreed that the ZG's reluctance to either decentralise the national budget, or to bestow adequate levels of authority to DCs to raise local, significantly militates against the strengthening of society through decentralisation. An official with the Chipinge DC, for example, argued that the critical elements of the decentralisation process which have seriously weakened society *vis-a-vis* the state is the fact that LGUs do not have any control over local economic activities, no meaningful decision-making authority, and little if any input into policy-making:

> Society is at the mercy of the ruling party and the state.
> People's demands are not met through the functioning of
> local authorities because these bodies do not have the
> means with which to implement the people's wishes. All
> decisions made by DCs, for example, have to be approved
> by the CG before they are implemented.[26]

Officials were, however, agreed that, generally, the ZG has the interests of the people at the local level at heart, and that the voices of local people has often been heard by the CG on various issues. Nevertheless, the fact remains that society has been weakened by the nature of the process of decentralisation which was initially geared to the creation of a one-party state in Zimbabwe. In the Matabeleland South Province, an official in the District Administrator's office insisted that, to all intents and purposes, Zimbabwe is basically, a *de facto* one party state in which the state has, necessarily become stronger and society weaker.

Asked whether society has not demonstrated that it can also make use of decentralisation to facilitate its resistance to unpopular or unacceptable government policies and programmes, officials were of the view that only grossly repugnant policies and programmes, such as certain models of land resettlement, have been resisted by the people with enough vigour to force the CG to respond in a positive way to the people's wishes. There are, however, many other issues on which the strong state has managed to make use of decentralisation to implement some of its less popular policies and programmes.

Impact of Decentralisation on Democracy

Crook and Manor (1991:24) argue that the presence of democracy is not a necessary part of the definition of decentralisation. They, however concede that the inclusion of democracy in the decentralisation process significantly influences the way the system will operate. The inclusion of democracy in the decentralisation process necessarily entails the need to effectively and genuinely distribute political power among local institutions. In some countries, the democratic elements of decentralisation begin and end with popular participation in the election of local representatives. This is unfortunate because local democracy can contribute a lot more to decentralisation and LG than is achieved through periodic popular elections. Apart from satisfying the legitimate political aspirations of subgroups and ethnically distinct regions, local democracy tends to have an educative effect on the people's representatives at the local level as they participate in decentralised, democratic institutions:

> Participation in such institutions is supposed to enhance civic consciousness and political maturity. People learn more quickly when they have to take responsibility for the decisions of local officials. They obtain an invaluable training in resource allocation. Thus a close association is perceived between local political institutions and political development . . . Such an education should ultimately enrich government at the centre as better trained politicians emerge from the grassroots (Smith, 1985:188).

Democratic decentralisation, when effectively implemented, should enable the people's representatives to effectively carry out three critical functions within the LG system. First, they should be able to meaningfully represent their 'constituencies' by making the local council aware of the needs, requests, demands and suggestions of their people. They should also defend, support and basically 'sell' these demands and needs to their colleagues in council and to district administrators, donor agencies and NGOs. Thus, as elected representatives, councillors should be concerned about the interests and welfare of their people. The representative function is best performed, not only by regularly attending council and committee meetings, but also by forging effective contacts and conducting consultations with members of the community in order to know their needs and proposed solutions to development and governance problems. A councillor's ability to favourably influence council on issues pertaining to his local area is largely determined by his performance of the representative function. Further, the effectiveness with which councillors carry out the representative function is critically dependent on whether the local council is operationally democratic or merely a democratically elected body which operates in a bureaucratic fashion. It is the contention of this study, based on the findings of field research, that in Zimbabwe, the DCs tend to fall in the latter category.

The second critical function which can be enhanced by the existence of fully-fledged democratic institutions at the local level is the deliberative function. This function is closely related to the representative function in that an elected representative of the people should not only consult with the people he represents on local problems and related issues, but he should also actively participate both in the deliberations of the VIDCOs and WADCOs, as well as in those of the DC.

A representative who attends a DC or committee meeting simply to collect his 'sitting allowance' at the end of the meeting, without having actively participated in the deliberations of the council is neglecting his duty as a democratically elected representative of the people. Council can only make favourable decisions on matters of interest or concern to a councillor's community if the councillor vigorously debates the issues with his colleagues and effectively represents his electorate's case. Democratic decentralisation enhances the performance of the deliberative function in that it is the right, and indeed, the duty, of every representative of the people to speak on whatever business is before the council. Further, democracy would also ensure that the views of every member are respected and taken into consideration when decisions are finally made. Available evidence seems to indicate that, in the areas under study, most of the people's representatives have grown weary of effectively performing the deliberative function for various reasons. Perhaps, the major inhibition to councillors' performance of the deliberative function is the DCs' lack of resources for the implementation of people initiated development plans and projects. Brand (1991:88) has noted in relation to VIDCOs and WADCOs in Centenary:

> What of the intention that VIDCOs and WADCOs should
> contribute to district, and eventually provincial plans through
> local project identification? Expectations in this regard
> were clearly unrealistic . . . There is not much point in
> repeating such an exercise, since it has little influence on
> what subsequently happens or does not happen in the

districts. Villagers get impatient with needs or project identification exercises. A headman in Mzarabani (Centenary) commented acidly to me, "Once it has been written down, it disappears without trace."

The third and final critical function of councillors at the grassroots level is the control function. As democratically elected members of local authorities, councillors have a governance role which requires that they effectively control both the staff and the physical resources and facilities of their DCs. Councillors are grassroots-based politicians who are expected to make wide-ranging decisions on how local resources are to be used. These decisions should be made within the parameters determined by statutory law. The findings of this study indicate that, at least in the districts under study, DCs have little control over both the officials of the DC and the district administration, and over other council resources. The major reasons for this anomalous situation is, once again the dominant role played by the CG through the DA and his officials, and the fact that DCs are over-dependent on the financial support they receive from the CG.

A significant number of officials of both the DCs and the district administration indicated that decentralisation in the post-1980 period has resulted in the strengthening of democracy at the local level in Zimbabwe. Some of the reasons they gave in support of this claim included:

- the grassroots people now have the right to democratically elect their own representatives without undue interference from the state;

- CG now takes into consideration the people's views on local issues when making decisions;

- Grassroots people are free to express their views on the way local development activities should be conducted, and they question public officials when they observe that local affairs are not being handled in the manner they will have recommended; and

- The people are now participating effectively in the development of their own areas, unlike during the colonial period.

These reasons were, however, contested by the majority of council and district administration officials who largely admitted that, on the face of it, decentralisation gives the impression that it has resulted in the strengthening of democracy at the grassroots level, but in reality, it has weakened it even further. A senior officer in the MLGRUD responsible for UCs, for example, argued that electoral apathy, poor attendance of meetings, and little interest in debating critical local issues are some of the main indicators of how decentralisation has weakened democracy at the local level, both in urban and in rural areas.[27] The officer further confirmed that appointed officials have more influence on policy and decision-making at the local level because of the nature of the post-independence LG system.

The General Secretary of the Rural Councils' Association of Zimbabwe asserted that the MLGRUD has not yet learnt how to decentralise power. This was confirmed by the Secretary General of the District Councils' Association who decried the weakness of most opposition parties in Zimbabwe which, if they were strong, could help 'tame the ruling party.' The same sentiments were echoed by several other respondents who gave the following as the major indications of how decentralisation has weakened democracy in Zimbabwe:

- decentralisation has not made government accountable to the people but only to itself;

- people's views are only taken into account in CG decision-making if they are not in conflict with the broad goals of government or the ruling party;

- the ruling party imposes candidates on the people and punishes members of the party who decide to stand for local elections as "independents";

- decentralisation does not result in the protection of minority groups and their interests unless they are members of the ruling party - women and youth leagues of ZANU/PF;

- whether they are employed by LAs or by the CG, public servants conform to the wishes and laid down procedures of the CG in their operations; they are not really influenced by the policies of LAs or by the people in their behaviour. The reason for this is that CG pays their salaries and also finances most of the DCs' activities;

- the fact that local leaders are not empowered to effectively deal with local issues, make local decisions and have them implemented, means that decentralisation has weakened democracy; and

- excessive CG control of LGUs make it impossible for decentralisation to strengthen democracy at the local level: the penetration of CG into the periphery through decentralisation has resulted in the visibility of CG at the detriment of both democracy and local autonomy.[28]

Most officials were of the opinion that both district and council administrators do not behave in accordance with the policies and wishes of the people. They stated that CG has laid down rules and regulations which govern the behaviour of public officials, which rules and regulations are not designed or implemented by the people. In fact, some respondents argued that officials sometimes make use of the excuse that they are not allowed to carry out certain functions by the government as a way of dismissing some of the private citizens' demands.[29] This has resulted in some of the focus groups interviewed for this study arguing that some of the post-1980 district and council administrators are not as well behaved as their pre-independence counterparts, which is a serious indictment inimical to the philosophical basis of decentralisation in a post-colonial society. This allegation was, however, only found in those districts where respondents had indicated that they were not satisfied with the performance of their DCs, or where they had indicated that they had not received any benefits from their DC but from the government.

Closely related to this finding was the respondents view regarding accountability of government. Although most officials felt that the post-independence government in Zimbabwe pays more attention to the voices of the people, they, nonetheless, were of the opinion that CG is largely accountable to itself rather than to the people in terms of its policies and actions. Some even argued that the large majority that the ruling party commands in the House of Parliament makes it possible for CG to 'steamroll' whatever legislation it wishes to see passed without necessarily accounting to the people through their representatives in Parliament. The majority of the officials interviewed asserted that the ZG is more accountable to the ruling party than to the people in most of its activities.

A good number of officials indicated that the dominance of the ruling party in decision-making, even at the local level, has meant that the people's wishes, particularly with regard to development priorities, are only accorded sympathetic consideration if they happen to coincide with the stated policies of both the CG and the ruling party.[30] Thus, in those areas where the ruling party does not receive popular support, such as in parts of Manicaland Province, this study found out that citizens are of the opinion that decentralisation has weakened democracy because none of the many decisions they have made have been implemented by their DCs.[31] This is certainly resulting in DCs becoming unpopular with the citizens, and the implications for political development can be negative, indeed.

The imposition of candidates preferred by the ruling party on certain wards, particularly in urban areas, has been the general practice of ZANU/PF for some time. Since 1985, however, ward residents have frequently rejected those party members they felt were not of their choice, or were not resident in their wards. Some candidates have sought to contest LG elections as independents, and incurred the wrath of the ruling party. A number of respondents argued that while the ruling party has a right to decide who it will support in any election, it is necessary that the local members of the party be allowed to make the initial decision without fear or favour. The 'punishment' meted out to 'independents' was therefore, viewed as a negation of democracy at the local level.

Some officials pointed out that both the PMDs and related legislation did not result in the creation of a LG system which adequately protects the rights and interests of minority groups that are not part and parcel of the ruling ZANU/PF party. The major minority groups within the ruling party are the women and the youth. Both of these groups are represented at all levels from the VIDCO to the PC. Experience has shown that, in practically all districts of Zimbabwe, the ZANU/PF Women's League and Youth League have been the only representatives of these minority groups.[32]

This has had the result of significantly marginalising minority groups which have no affiliation to the ruling party. This confirms the earlier assumption that the decentralisation structure was primarily conceived for the purposes of creating a one-party state in Zimbabwe. The recent disintegration of authoritarian regimes throughout Africa and beyond has not resulted in any significant revision of the LG system to correct these anomalies. Indeed, even the latest LG legislation which will result in the amalgamation of RCs and DCs makes provision for the minister of LG to appoint special interest groups' representatives at various levels of the structure. Respondents were largely agreed that the provision is likely to be used to ensure that the ruling party's own minority groups remain the only beneficiaries.

The majority of respondents indicated that the ZG commands a high level of legitimacy among the people, mainly, because it is the very first black majority government, and because it has significantly improved the lot of the ordinary citizens in both the rural and urban areas of Zimbabwe. The ZG has, since the attainment of national independence, improved roads, built new schools, clinics, hospitals and people's markets in various parts of the country. Most of these developmental activities were undertaken by CG itself rather than through LAs. Nonetheless, this has had the effect of influencing the local people to look upon the government as legitimate and genuinely interested in their welfare. But there is a sense in which this level of CG activity at the local level has jeopardised the chances of popular acceptance of local institutions since they cannot match CG's performance. As noted earlier, some respondents among the ordinary citizens argued that DCs are not appropriate for their areas because they do not provide them with as many benefits as the DA's office does.[33]

Most respondents were reluctant to link the legitimacy accorded the government to decentralisation and argued that CG is regarded as exercising excessive control over LAs, which severely restricts the level of autonomy of LAs to the barest minimum. A comparison of the responses from the districts under study reveals that in those districts where the DC is perceived by the general public as having performed effectively and efficiently, the majority of respondents attributed the legitimacy that is accorded to the ZG to decentralisation. But in districts where the citizens were dissatisfied with the performance of their DC, the majority of respondents were of the opinion that the government's legitimacy was largely based on factors other than decentralisation.

A councillor in the Chipinge District, for example, argued that decentralisation was not a factor in the determination of the legitimacy of the ZG because policies, projects and programmes implemented in the district were all of a top-down nature. Rather, the councillor asserted, the fact that the majority of the current government officials and national politicians were active participants in the liberation struggle is, probably the major factor. The apathy that pervades LG elections in most of Zimbabwe seems to attest to this assumption.

Impact of Political Parties on Decentralisation

Although the ruling ZANU/PF party has done all in its power to create a *de facto* one-party state in Zimbabwe, there are still no less than ten officially registered political parties in existence in the country. The merging of the former ZAPU/PF and ZANU/PF in December, 1987 resulted in the creation of a mammoth political party with support in virtually all regions of the country. That 'Unity Accord' between the two factions of the Patriotic Front of the liberation period was projected as denoting national unity and thereby creating a favourable climate for the institutionalisation of a *de jure* one-party state. The collapse of socialism and other forms of authoritarian regimes in Eastern Europe, Africa and other parts of the world, however, forced the ruling party in Zimbabwe to re-assess its intentions of creating a *de jure* one-party state. It is the contention of this study that ZANU/PF has now opted for a *de facto* one-party state in which it remains the only viable political party in the country. A number of policy measures can be identified which confirm this present position of the ruling party. Examples include:

* The shift from a ceremonial to an executive presidency in 1987;

* The abolition of a two chamber and adoption of a single chamber parliamentary system;

* The creation of the now defunct Ministry of Political Affairs which served as the 'secretariat' of the ruling party but which was financed by Treasury funds; and

* The passing of legislation approving the use of public funds to support political parties which have a minimum of fifteen representatives in Parliament.[34]

Further, the ruling party has been actively pursuing a policy of victimisation of political opponents as is evidenced by dismissals of individuals who had joined opposition political parties from boards of parastatals.[35] Another example is the designation of an opposition party leader's commercial farm for compulsory acquisition by the government on the flimsy excuse that he had allowed too many landless people to settle on the farm.[36] Several other examples could be mentioned,[37] but these few serve the purpose of demonstrating the ruling party's determination to create a *de facto* one-party system in Zimbabwe. This situation, obviously, has significant implications for decentralisation.

Almost all the respondents to the survey for this study indicated that political parties do make a significant difference to the way decentralised institutions operate. They, however, felt that the current political climate in Zimbabwe does not promote the participation of opposition political parties in LG affairs to any meaningful degree. An officer in the MLGRUD head office in Harare, for example, argued that support for opposition parties in the Manicaland and Matabeleland Provinces has sometimes resulted in the frustration of local people, and their alienation from LG activities. Further, CG has also not been very enthusiastic about undertaking LG activities in DC areas where the LGUs were dominated by members of opposition parties.[38]

The MLGRUD official further asserted that as currently structured, decentralisation poses a threat to multi-party politics in Zimbabwe because it is not designed to accommodate multi-party configurations.[39] The commonest example referred to by respondents in relation to this assertion was the representation of ZANU/PF women and youth Leagues in the WADCOs, VIDCOs and DCs. Some respondents also pointed out that the ruling party has little tolerance for any deviation from the party line in the operations of LGUs at all levels. This has the tendency of making LGUs virtually extensions of the ruling party at the expense of other parties and independent representatives of the people.

A slightly different dimension to the role of political parties in LG was highlighted in the Chipinge District where district administration officials claimed that, because of the strong support that the opposition ZANU (Ndonga) party has in the district, political party leaders are noted for mobilising people to oppose DC policies and projects but to support and participate in NGO initiated and funded ones. The surprising aspect of the matter is that all the members of the DC are, presumably, residents of the same district, who must have been elected by the people into the DC. Officials explained that the majority of the councillors fell out of favour with the people when it was perceived that they (the councillors) were implementing CG policies, programmes and projects without question. The politicisation of decentralisation in favour of the ruling party has, thus, weakened the role of political parties, other than the ruling party, in the LG system in Zimbabwe.[40] This, in turn, has had a negative effect on democracy since political parties are, normally, essential for a healthy democratic political system.

A member of the Manicaland PC[41] expressed trepidation at the non-participation of other political parties in LG affairs. He agreed that most of the opposition parties were afraid of being victimised by the ruling party should they actively push for changes in the LG system which currently favours the ruling party. He urged that the participation of opposition parties would enable LGUs to depart from the current situation where they are conditioned to conform to the ruling ZANU/PF's wishes, sometimes, at the expense of those of the people.

Every political party, once in power, will seek to retain that power for as long as possible. The experience of many an African country indicates that national political leaders have a tendency of devising all sorts of ways of extending their tenure of office even if this may entail changing the 'rules of the game' during their legitimate term of office. The ruling ZANU/PF party of Zimbabwe is no exception to this practice. The proliferation of political parties in Zimbabwe since the advent of national independence has exacerbated the ruling party's penchant for survival and self-perpetuation. This may explain why, despite the abandonment of "the road to socialism" in the early nineties, the ZG has not bothered to make any significant changes to the decentralisation and LG systems in Zimbabwe since they serve its purposes of longevity of tenure. Sadly, the implications for both meaningful decentralisation and democracy, as well as for national socio-economic and political development are necessarily negative.

The Effect of Decentralisation on Civil Society

It has already been stated that decentralisation in Zimbabwe has been characterised by excessive CG controls over local institutions. This has had the effect of constraining civil society as is evidenced by the predominance of CG influence on what development activities DCs can undertake, and on the decision-making processes at the local level. This study, however, found out that civil society has not been entirely inhibited from participating in development although its involvement has largely been supported by NGOs rather than by government or its agencies.

Asked whether decentralisation in Zimbabwe encourages or promotes civil society, a senior official in the MLGRUD pointed out that, as currently structured, decentralisation tends to be selective on the elements of civil society that it promotes. The selection is based on the relations that civil groups have, or are likely to have, with the different political parties in a given locality. The leadership of civil groups is also a critical factor in the kind of support and latitude that a civil group may be able to receive from, or allowed by decentralised institutions, and the CG. The MLGRUD official, for example, stated that his ministry tends to 'discourage and frustrate' Residents' Associations because they are usually alleged to incite their members to oppose the policies and activities of LAs: 'They are highly instrumental in resisting urban council policies and in opposing most policy changes.'[42]

The Chipinge DC Senior Executive Officer (SEO) was of the opinion that decentralisation in Zimbabwe does promote the formation of autonomous bodies which are free to lobby government but, in most cases, these groups meet with very little success because CG ignores them unless they are formed within the ruling ZANU/PF party.[43] Another respondent in the same district asserted that decentralisation neither promotes nor frustrates the formation of autonomous civil groups, but there is a tendency among elements within the ruling party, to suspect that every newly formed group might convert itself into a political party which could compete with or criticise the ruling ZANU/PF party.

This was echoed by a Midlands Province administrative officer who, agreeing that minority groups have largely been marginalised as a result of decentralisation, also alleged that the ruling party projects the view that after the creation of VIDCOs and WADCOs, there is really no need for any new groups among the people; everyone is expected to take their demands, requests and suggestions to the CG through existing structures, which are often projected as 'people's institutions.'[44]

Civil society plays a crucial role in the development of a society. Ideally, decentralisation should be aimed at promoting the formation of autonomous groups among citizens at the local level in order to reduce the citizen's dependence on government and centrally distributed resources. In Zimbabwe, however, there seems to be a reluctance on the part of CG to facilitate the development of autonomous bodies which, it is feared, may some day challenge the ruling elite for political power and other resources that are currently the preserve of the ruling party. The implications of this approach are obviously inimical to both democracy and development. Some of the consequences of this approach are: a high level of public lethargy in relation to LGU and CG initiated development and governance activities, including participation in elections; excessive dependence on handouts from government and donor agencies on the part of the people; and increasing popularity of NGOs as the only institutions that have the people's needs at heart, and which can bring about meaningful improvements to the living standards of the people.[45]

6
The Political Dimension of Decentralisation: Citizens' View

In an earlier section of this study, reference was made to the rationale for decentralisation, and it was pointed out that one of the main objectives is to facilitate the provision of goods and services by LGUs, to the citizens of a locality without excessive interference from CG. Thus the functions of LGUs are expected to be geared towards the needs of the people, and to be determined and prioritised by the local people themselves. A further objective of decentralisation is to bring government closer to the people. This implies that decentralisation should result in significantly improved public access to decentralised structures of government and LG. The leadership, and other personnel, of decentralised institutions plays a crucial role in the execution or realisation of both these objectives.

This section of the study will discuss the views of the citizens of the districts under study in relation to the three aspects of decentralisation mentioned above - functions, access to government or to public services, and the nature of the leadership in charge of decentralised institutions. Most of the views discussed below are of focus groups interviewed in the target areas of the study. A striking feature of the views is their uniformity in a given council area for almost all the groups interviewed. Here again, the performance of the DC seems to have been the critical factor in determining the responses that were given to interviewers in the respective areas. It may be useful to note that this section did not focus on the developmental but mainly on the political functions of DCs.

DCs' Performance of their Functions
The highest level of recorded negative responses to the performance of a DC among the seven districts was gathered in the Kadoma District. The peri-urban nature of this district may account for the kind of responses that were provided since urban areas tend to have a significantly higher level of political consciousness than rural areas, at least in Zimbabwe. For example, a focus group of ten people in the Kadoma district maintained that their DC does not effectively carry out its functions, whether they be political or developmental. They accused their councillors of failing to convey the people's needs and decisions to higher authorities. Two other groups in the same district, but

different wards, expressed the same sentiments, and charged that their councillors are unable to perform the representative function effectively.[46] Some respondents alleged that their representatives were 'sitting pretty' and were not bothered about the suffering of those who placed them into office.[47]

A contrary view was recorded in the Gwanda district where members of a focus group expressed satisfaction with their DC. Citizens pointed out that their DC was instrumental in the settling of disputes between peasant farmers in the CAs and those in the RAs regarding grazing areas for their livestock.[48] Almost all the members of the focus group knew the names of their DC executives because they had frequent contacts with them during the resolution of the dispute.

Thus, another factor determining the citizens' appreciation of their DC may be the magnitude of the issues that the DC has, at any time, had to deal with, and whether it was successful in its efforts or not. Asked about the performance of the three critical functions of people's representatives - deliberative, control and representative - three focus groups in the Gwanda area indicated that their representatives performed very effectively the deliberative and the representative functions, but had not performed effectively the control function. The respondents also argued in support of their representatives and pointed out that CG's excessive controls over LGUs make it difficult, if not illegal, for the people's representatives to try and control DCs.

It would, therefore, appear that in districts which have experienced significant problems which required the organisation and mobilisation of the people, and where the DCs have been instrumental in spearheading the citizens' position on the issues, the focus groups tend to have a positive view of the effectiveness of their DCs. On the other hand, in districts where there has not been any seriously contentious issue, the DC, although it has, basically, performed its 'normal' tasks to some degree, has largely been castigated as politically ineffective.

Accessibility of DCs to the Public

Here again, Kadoma ranks as the district in which the citizens are most dissatisfied with the level of access they have to their own DC. Two of the three focus groups interviewed in this district indicated that people are often sent away from the DC offices when they have complaints, or when they wish to report certain matters, or obtain certain services.[49] The members of both focus groups alleged that officials always ask them to 'follow procedures' but in reality they will be fearing for their jobs; they are afraid of criticism from ordinary citizens. The third group of seven people was opposed to the DC implementing, largely, CG's preferred programmes and projects without consulting them first. The group was highly critical of what the members called the dictatorial approach of both their own DC and the DA's office: 'We have never met DC officials to tell them what we want or do not want, but they dictate matters to us.'[50]

Two of the focus groups indicated that they had never asked for council records to examine them because they did not know that they had a right to do so. They were, however, sceptical that they would ever be allowed to examine the DC records since they were regarded as 'uneducated.' One member in the third group indicated that he had once asked to examine the records but was informed by DC officials that records were only made available to CG auditors and not to ordinary citizens.

This study found out that citizens in practically all the areas under study were not aware that they had the right to ask for and examine DC records. This is obviously a failure on the part of the people's representatives to educate and inform their electors on this vital provision. Indeed, in the Kadoma District, respondents claimed that they had more access to public officials of both the DC and the DA's office prior to 1980 than they have now. This is indisputably, a serious indictment against both the DC and the district administration.[51]

Most of the sentiments expressed above were echoed by the Gokwe focus groups, who also claimed that they never receive any feedback from their representatives on issues they will have raised with them. Claiming that they had better access to public offices in the district prior to independence than now, the Gokwe focus groups further indicated that they had much better access to both the VIDCOs and the WADCOs than to the DC and the district administration. The problem was, however, that both the VIDCOs and the WADCOs did not have the resources with which to solve some of the citizens' problems.

In the Chipinge District, focus groups indicated that there was no variation in the accessibility of DC and DA's offices from what they had before the attainment of national independence. They further charged that both the DC and the DA's offices were suffering from 'too much bureaucracy.'[52] The only access they had to these institutions was either through their councillors, or through their chief. The Maungwe District focus groups claimed the same bureaucratic problems with their DC, and further alleged that it takes more than a single visit to these offices to get the officials to serve a citizen. One of the Maungwe focus groups insisted that the pre-independence situation was a lot better because today's officials are 'harsh and impolite.'[53]

In all the target districts, citizens were emphatic that their representatives could improve on their consultation and feedback activities. Councillors for their part argued that the majority of their people do not always turn up for meetings when they are called. Councillors further alleged that they face considerable transportation difficulties when they try to visit their wards since they are not provided with bicycles with the DC. The WADCOs and VIDCOs do not have the necessary resources for the purchase of bicycles for their councillors. Thus although the majority of the focus groups in all the areas felt that the deliberative and the representative functions were fairly carried out by their representatives, they were of the opinion that more could be done. They, however, were completely dissatisfied about the councillors' inability to perform the control function over the DCs. This they attributed to the strong hand of the ZG over local affairs.

The Role of Leadership in the Performance of DCs

The leadership of an institution plays a crucial role in determining the programme, doctrine, linkages, outputs and mode of operation of the institution. The doctrine of the organisation will determine the kinds of programmes and projects that the institution will undertake in order to be productive, while the linkages, which must be forged and effectively managed by the leadership, will determine the kind of resources that the institution will be able to obtain from its environment, as well as facilitate the adoption of the institution's outputs by its clients and other elements within the environment.

The leadership, in order to effectively manage the affairs of the institution as briefly outlined above, must have certain attributes or qualities which are appropriate for the performance of their tasks in the management of the institution. Authorities are not entirely agreed on whether leadership qualities are in-born, acquired through learning, or, as it were, thrust upon one by sheer social circumstances. It would not be within the scope of this study to delve into the intricacies of the debate about this controversial issue. Suffice it to note here that the majority of the qualities of good leaders that the respondents identified were based on the respondents' experience, mainly with their current leaders. In other words they seemed to identify those qualities that were the direct opposites of what they perceived their leaders to be and argued that those were the acceptable qualities of good leadership. Respondents were asked to identify some of the attributes that they considered to be crucial for the effective management of the affairs of their DCs. They were also asked to indicate whether their current leadership possessed these qualities or not. Focus groups in the target districts came up with the following leadership qualities:

A good leader must:
- listen to the people;
- not distort information;
- fulfil election promises;
- be honest with the people;
- represent the people's wishes;
- not be a puppet of the DC or the DA;
- provide timely feedback to the people;
- be fair to all and not favour some people;
- be fair to all areas in distribution of projects.

Most of these qualities of good leadership were discussed by the focus groups prior to their being agreed upon. In five of the seven districts under study, focus groups alleged that their representatives did not have all of these attributes. In the remaining two districts, the respondents argued that while some of their leaders possessed some of these qualities, they lacked the courage to confront government officials whom they claimed refuse to take the people's grievances to higher authorities.

Focus groups were largely well informed about the procedures of removing incompetent representatives from office. In almost all the districts, the groups admitted that there is nothing they can do to remove the representative from office before the next election. They however, were agreed that an incompetent representative runs the risk of not being re-elected in subsequent council elections. In one district, however, the majority of a ten member focus group conceded that some dubious representatives have built such a formidable following that they always get re-elected.[54] In one focus group, an articulate member stated that an ineffective representative should be asked to step down voluntarily before the expiry of his term of office, but if he refuses, then the people should be urged not to vote for him in the following round of elections.

The Kadoma focus groups were quite vicious about their current leadership which they categorised as worse than the colonial LG and district administrators. They accused their representatives of not standing for the people's rights and interests. They further argued that their leaders do not promote popular participation in the activities of the DC. Two groups of ten people each and one of seven gave strangely identical responses to this issue of leadership qualities.

In Gokwe, however, the respondents were of the view that although some of their leaders do not have these qualities, they are much better than the pre-1980 colonial ones since they sometimes pay some attention to what the people say. They further suggested that even the leaders that do not have these qualities could acquire them through training. The Chivi and Maungwe focus groups also expressed the same views, particularly on the need for training people's representatives.[55]

The views discussed above highlight a number of problems which seem to beset decentralisation in Zimbabwe. The majority of people in the districts under study are not satisfied with the performance of their DCs in terms of both their own expectations and the normal functions of local institutions. Accessibility of DCs to the public seems to have deteriorated in comparison with the pre-independence situation. The majority of the leaders of DCs are unable to provide effective leadership because they lack appropriate attributes. Consequently leadership - citizens relations are considerably poor in some of the target districts. Procedures for the removal or recall of incompetent leaders do not allow for the removal of a leader during his term of office. This is a critical weakness of the LG system in Zimbabwe, one which needs to be addressed if decentralisation is to have a positive impact on both development and democracy. It seems evident that, as currently structured, decentralisation in Zimbabwe cannot lead to meaningful political development among the people at the grassroots level.

7
Decentralisation for Social Control

Continuity of 'Separate Development'

The colonial LG system in Zimbabwe was deliberately designed to facilitate the provision of social, economic and political benefits to the colonizers, the dominant white racial group, and to facilitate effective social control of the majority Africans. The system was closely linked to the forcible acquisition of fertile, good rainfall land from the Africans, and the distribution of this land among white settlers and European private companies. This link was important since it significantly alienated the majority Africans from the colonialists and encouraged Africans to actively participate in the liberation struggle which eventually resulted in the attainment of national independence in 1980.

But the legal framework within which Zimbabwe was 'granted' national independence had been cleverly devised by the former colonialists to forestall rapid removal of the pillars of racial segregation, particularly pertaining to the acquisition and distribution of land by the new ZG. The LG system which resulted after a number of peripheral reforms to the colonial system, though devoid of the racial factor as part of the criteria for determining the composition of councils, residential areas and systems of land occupation, only managed to make 'separate development' change the colour of its garb. The reforms did not end 'separate development,' they only redefined it according to socio-economic statuses of the various groups of citizens residing in the various parts of the country. Terms like 'high density' versus 'low density' urban areas clearly denote a socio-economic status, while the dichotomous relationship between urban and rural areas has persisted in spite of attempts to "urbanize" the rural areas by the creation of, largely unsuccessful, Growth Points and Service Centres.

Other evidence of the continuity of the colonial system of LG include the continued disenfranchisement of farm labourers residing on commercial farms; the continued dominant role of the District Administrator over both deconcentrated and devolved LG bodies; attempts at the restoration of traditional leaders' colonial authority and responsibilities, largely for the purpose of facilitating the effective social control of the rural masses; the creation of an economically and politically weak LG system which depends on the goodwill of the CG to survive since it lacks viable authority either to make decisions or to raise and allocate local resources for the benefit of citizens at the local level.

State Penetration of the Local Domain

The post-independence LG system in Zimbabwe was deliberately designed to serve the purpose of creating a one-party state, with the ruling ZANU/PF party as the one party. The world-wide disenchantment with authoritarian regimes and the popular demands for democracy and multi-party politics in most of Africa and the world meant that the ruling party could not proceed with its grand self-perpetuation plans without facing serious local and international ostracism. The resort to a *de facto* one-party system was, the second best option and this study contends that the current regime in Zimbabwe is pursuing this option. The policy implications of these developments for the LG system in Zimbabwe are necessarily a negation of the notions of democratic decentralization, beneficiary participation in development, and the pursuit of the creation of a strong state at the expense of the weak society.

Indeed, the post-colonial LG system has resulted in the penetration of the state right down to the village level, but only in terms of the visibility of CG rather than in terms of any meaningful empowerment of the citizens at the village, ward and district levels. The lack of resources of all kinds and the fact that real decisions have to be made by CG public officials is a clear indication that, as currently constituted, the LG system in Zimbabwe, outside of the urban areas, hardly qualifies as local government; it is more of local administration than the colonial system which it replaced. The views of both appointive and elective officials at the district and provincial levels, and those of the citizens of the seven districts under this study confirm this assertion to a considerable extent.

The state's penetration to the lower levels must, therefore, be seen as having a hidden agenda, which, this study would argue, is the self-preservation of the ruling party, ZANU/PF. Both the structure and the various provisions governing LG operations confirm this assertion, and the findings of this study further corroborate the evidence of previous works in this area. This usurpation of the state by the ruling party has had serious negative implications for civil society, which finds itself hamstrung as the ruling party suspects civil groups outside the party to be potential competitors in the rat-race for scarce local resources. Political apathy during elections, nonchalance, if not outright resistance or hostility towards participating in LG activities, as discussed in this study, are but a few indicators of the general dissatisfaction that the general public at the district and lower level have with the current LG system in Zimbabwe.

Amalgamation: Marginalization of the Weak Voice and The Reinforcement of the Exit Option

This study has noted that as a further way of removing the racial factor from the LG system after independence, the ZG, in 1988 promulgated the Rural District Councils Act, which *inter alia*, seeks to amalgamate RC and DCs into RDCs. The exercise is currently in progress but a few remarks can be made on the likely implications for citizens of the former DC areas. The rationale for amalgamating the RCs and DCs goes beyond the removal of the racial factor from the LG system. It is also a way of reducing CG financial and other support for LGUs and facilitating the raising of local revenues by LGUs themselves for their own development. This is in line with the ESAP which has this approach to the reduction of CG expenditure as one of its conditionalities.

The resistance levelled at the amalgamation process by white commercial farmers in most of the LSCFs was mainly based on the realization that, to all intends and purposes, RCs were being forced to subsidize the development of CAs which are generally known to be extremely limited in both technical and financial resources. A major requirement of the amalgamation process is that, unlike prior to the implementation of the RDC Act, citizens of the RDCs will be required to pay a development levy annually. Preliminary investigations indicate that the majority of citizens are vehemently opposed to the imposition of this levy, and are arguing that they cannot afford to pay it. Although the levy has been on the books of most DCs for years, there had been little effort to enforce its collection. RDCs, however, need to actively enforce the collection of this revenue if they are to operate effectively. CG has made it clear that the support that local authorities receive from central coffers will be progressively reduced over time.

One of the several implications of this situation is likely to be further marginalization of the majority of the peasants as they will opt out of active participation in local affairs because of lack of both financial and technical resources. RDCs are expected to have members from both the DCs and the RCs in their composition. CG has made it clear that citizens should elect individual citizens who are knowledgeable and can understand government policies. Indeed, this was a way of asking the peasants to elect only literate and fairly "successful" poeple as their representatives in the RDCs. The result will be that the local elites will be the major beneficiaries of the new RDCs, and the peasants will largely recede to their pre-1980 situation - detached from the state, voiceless, and permanently pursuing the exit option. The implications for democracy can only be negative under these circumstances.

Decentralization will, once again, result in increased benefits for the more fortunate, whether black or white, and the poor will remain, largely, outside the captured state.

Consequences of Decentralization in Post-Colonial Zimbabwe

Although decentralization is easily conceivable as crucial for the effective administration and management of local affairs and local development activities, it is basically a political decision aimed at serving, primarily political goals. For the most part, these political goals are determined by the ruling elite from a defined ideological position. The post-colonial decentralization efforts in Zimbabwe were purposed to facilitate the primary goal of ensuring the perpetuation and dominance of the ruling ZANU/PF party as the only viable and legal political party in the country. To a considerable extent, this goal has been largely achieved, but at a considerable cost to national development and democratic governance.

This study has amply demonstrated that the 'winners' in the decentralization process in Zimbabwe are largely the ruling ZANU/PF party, central government and its locally-based bureaucrats, and selected or favoured regions in the country. The ordinary citizens at the grassroots level are, generally, the "losers" who now perceive decentralization as purely serving the interests of the political party and the bureaucracy, rather than their own. NGOs are also major winners of the decentralization process since they have been able to make use of the LG structures to facilitate their won activities, especially through the use of these structures for the mobilization of the local masses for development activities. In relation to state-society relations, it is only correct to conclude, given the findings discussed above, that the state is the clear winner while society has significantly been weakened, to the extent that it now depends on the goodwill of the former for its survival, particularly in relation to financial and technical resources for local development.

Decentralization in Zimbabwe has not resulted in the evolution of a meaningfully democratic political system. The original agenda for the institution of decentralization - the creation of a socialist one-party state - had not been officially revised or abandoned. Rather, the pursuit of this objective has now taken on a more subtle, and therefore, more malevolent approach, given the 'new international political order' (NIPO), which is antagonistic to both socialism and the one-party authoritarian regime type. Thus, rather than result in the empowerment of the people at the local level, decentralization has created a highly dependent local mass which looks up to CG for basically, all its needs. CG has maintained a tight stranglehold on national resources by

Table III

Status of Respondent	Comments
VIDCO members	VIDCOs should be given more power to deal with issues of a local nature; The village committee is frustrated, issues we have raised have not been attended to; some members have already left the committee; Most of our projects are lying idle because we have no funds for implementing them; We need help from the WADCO and the DC and government because we have no skills in implementing our projects; We want quick responses to our suggestions; at the moment we get no feedback at all; VIDCOs need more training. They are almost useless now; nowadays no one recognizes them. You have actually reminded me that there is something like a VIDCO, I had forgotten all about it yet I am secretary of the VIDCO;
WADCO members	Yes WADCOs are useful for participation but the government should give WADCO members an allowance; They are useful because we are all villagers and can express our views freely. Government should provide WADCO members with bicycles so that we can effectively co-ordinate development activities; Some of our projects have been turned down because of lack of funds. This has created tension between the councillor and the people;

The people's participation is greatly enhanced but the higher officials ignore our suggestions;

People are reluctant to attend meetings. The term of office of WADCO members should be limited because incumbent members are reluctant to vacate office;

People tend to pay more attention to traditional leaders than to VIDCO and WADCO members. Chiefs and headmen should be included in these structures.

Central and Local Government Officials	Public participation in development has increased as a result of VIDCOs and WADCOs;
	Participation in public policy has increased, particularly in the health sector;
	People are building schools, clinics, and dams with government only providing technical advice;
	People identify their own needs and projects; they should explore ways and means of raising funds for these projects;
	Participation has only been meaningful through VIDCOs and WADCOs in NGO funded projects. Projects submitted to provincial and national institutions have yet to be implemented;
	These structures have not been useful in policy formulation because it is all top-down in this country.

Notes

1. Interview with the Matabeleland South Provincial Administrator. The signing of the Unity Accord resulted in the end of the Dissident War and the resumption of normal government activities in Matabeleland.
2. For elaboration on these objectives and benefits of decentralisation see, for example, Smith, 1985:3-12; Otzen, 1988:14-16; and L'Oeil, 71-72.
3. African Councils were initially called Native Councils, then later changed to African Councils, then to District Councils up to the attainment of national independence.
4. This Act was preceded by the Municipal Act (1930).
5. A number of other pieces of legislation facilitated the carrying out of most of these functions by UCs. For example, the Services Levy Act (Chapter 78) enabled UCs to impose a levy on employers of African labour, which funds were used to subsidise housing and transport services for Africans in urban areas (Palley, 1966 : 630).
6. See for example, Helmsing et al., 1991; Mutizwa-Mangiza, 1990; De Valk and Wekwete, 1990; and Wekwete, 1988. All of these authors are, or have been members of the Department of Rural and Urban Planning at the University of Zimbabwe.
7. All urban areas in Zimbabwe are still divided into high-density (former African) and low-density (former European) areas. As the terms imply, most middle and low income earners reside in high-density areas. This, obviously, has implications for democratic representation of the citizens residing in the two different areas.
8. SALA stands for the Swedish Association of Local Authorities. Members of this association were invited to study the local government system in Zimbabwe and assist the ZG in efforts to reform it. After many years of research and reports, the ZG is reported to have rejected most of the SALA recommendations.
9. The University of Zimbabwe is located in this ward. Since 1988, the UZ students had demonstrated against the ZG for various reasons. Both these demonstrations and subsequent police interventions resulted in considerable conscientisation of the citizens in this ward.
10. For example, in the Mount Pleasant case cited above, the winner of the election received a total of only 64 votes. The ward has more than five thousand rate payers and lodgers.

11. See for example, Brand, (1991:79-96); Mutizwa-Mangiza, (1986:153-175); and De Valk and Wekwete, (1990).
12. See for example, Wekwete, (1991:168-170); and PDSP/MLGRUD, (1992:10).
13. This was a study of the local government reforms since the attainment of national independence. That study covered elements of local government beyond the major focus of this study - decentralisation.
14. Interview with senior MLGRUD officials. They, in fact, argued that the President is not required, by law, to consult anyone on these appointments. The truth is that he consults the relevant provincial cadres of his party.
15. The MLGRUD/SALA Report indicates that DCs were receiving about 95% of their financial resources from the ZG in 1986, and that the situation was still basically the same by 1990.
16. The RDC Act (1988) Section 60 (1) (b) provides for the inclusion in the RDC of all chairmen of committees established by the RDC.
17. The Secretary to the District Councils Association further indicated that most citizens of district councils are reluctant to participate in government initiated development activities after a good agricultural season. In his view, the food-for-work approach to beneficiary participation in development is likely to have negative implications for unpaid citizen participation in self-help and other community development activities.
18. This was confirmed by a focus group in the same district. The group cited examples of local residents who were victimised by the local ruling party leadership for various reasons, including supporting opposition parties.
19. Interview with an administrative officer in the District Administrator's office, Gwanda. He further pointed out that to a large extent, DCs are insensitive to local needs because they are preoccupied with having to fulfill specific bureaucratic requirements.
20. The official MLGRUD structure does not indicate this position, but a number of district officers throughout the country claimed that they were Assistant or Deputy District Administrators. A deputy Secretary at the Ministry headquarters confirmed that the position does not officially exist on the ministry's establishment.
21. It is government policy that local people should benefit from the meat and hunting license fees generated in their local area. The policy is intended to facilitate community preservation of wildlife, and to reduce unlicensed game hunting and trapping of wildlife.
22. This statement was issued prior to the release of the PMDS but after the

ZG had committed itself to the programme of accelerated rural development under a socialist mode of production.

23. Ian Smith was the leader of the minority Rhodesia Front Party which declared UDI in 1965. It is considered a serious insult for any administrator or public officer to be accused of behaving like Ian Smith's administrators. That respondents stated that Smith's administrators were better indicates the way they feel about current district administrators.

24. Interview with a DA of a district in the Midlands Province, who insisted that both deconcentration and devolution have not yet been implemented in Zimbabwe.

25. A few of the respondents were confused by the term "strong state" and gave responses which indicated that decentralisation had caused the state to become weaker as there were too many decision-makers at the various levels of local and national governance. The majority of these were CG officials at the district level.

26. The official further asserted that as a direct consequence of this arrangement, many local people only appealed to the DC in times of dire need such as under drought conditions. This has seriously undermined the effectiveness of the DC, and has alienated the people from their local leaders.

27. Interview with a Deputy Secretary in the MLGRUD head office. He further argued that even in big urban areas, the number of citizens who actually participate in local government affairs continue to diminish each year. Very few people bother to even attend council meetings, or question their representatives on any of the council's decisions.

28. Based on the responses of district administrators and employees of DCs. Members of local authority associations were largely of the opinion that unless very strong opposition parties emerged in Zimbabwe, and participated in grassroots politics, there would be very little chance of meaningful democratic decentralisation under the present LG system.

29. This was stated in an interview with three officials of the Matabeleland South Provincial administration who also stressed the fact that council officials have no choice but to comply with CG directives since it is the CG which provides most of the finances needed by DCs.

30. One respondent in the Matabeleland South Province argued that the Minister and the Permanent Secretary in the MLGRUD have too much power: "District Councils end up being mere advisory bodies on local matters".

31. An Administrative Officer in Gwanda, for example, argued that decentralisation in Zimbabwe has resulted in what he termed "controlled democracy" since the CG has the final say on all major decisions.

32. The Gokwe DA surprised us by stating: "In Gokwe, we do not have minority groups, so that question does not apply to us here . . . . we also do not have autonomous groups".

33. Interview with a focus group in Kadoma, which also suggested that their DC should be merged with the DA's office so that it can perform its tasks more effectively. The same sentiments were also expressed by a focus group in the Chivi District.

34. ZANU/PF is the only political party which qualifies for the use of Treasury funds under this legislation. Opposition political parties have only three members in the current Parliament. Soon after the passing of this legislation. The ruling party "awarded" itself $20 million (US$3,33m) of Treasury funds.

35. A member of the Board of Directors of the Cold Storage Commission who recently joined the Democratic Forum Party of Zimbabwe was asked to step down from the Board on the grounds, denied by the ZG, that he was a member of an opposition party.

36. Rev. Ndabaningi Sithole's Churu Farm was designated by the ZG in 1993 for compulsory acquisition, purportedly for the resettlement of landless peasants. Sithole is the President of the opposition ZANU (Ndonga) party which is the popular party in the Chipinge District.

37. A further example, mentioned by a senior official in the MLGRUD, was the dismissal of the Manicaland Provincial Administrator on the allegation that he was seen talking to a leader of an opposition party at a filling station in Mutare.

38. This situation was most prevalent in the Matabeleland Provinces prior to the signing of the Unity Accord in 1987. The situation has improved significantly in this area since then, but remains largely the same in the Chipinge District, where the ruling party ZANU/PF has consistently failed to attract meaningful popular support.

39. The same views were expressed by a member of the Manicaland Provincial Council who felt that the whole LG structure in Zimbabwe is a carbon copy of the ZANU/PF party structure. It must, therefore discourage multi-party politics in order to survive.

40. An official of the Midlands Provincial Administration asserted that Zimbabwe is, virtually a one-party state, so the only political party that

has any impact on decentralisation is the ruling party. In the Midlands Province, for example, only one DC, (Mashambazhou) has a few independent councillors.

41. This Manicaland PC member is also DC chairman for a district which is not included in the seven districts under study. A member of an opposition party, the respondent was unwilling to be quoted *verbatim* nor to have his name disclosed. This further underlines the "fear" that pervades even community leaders when faced with a possibility of ZANU/PF retaliation.

42. Interview with the Deputy Secretary responsible for Urban Councils in the MLGRUD. He also argued that some Residents' Associations have become fora for opposing national government policies, especially among white residents of some (unnamed) urban areas.

43. He gave the examples of various regional development associations which have had little success in influencing government policies and proposed development and governance activities throughout Zimbabwe. He further argued that the only ones which seem to have made any impact on government policy are those that are patronised by top level businessmen, national politicians and administrators.

44. The same sentiments were expressed by an administrative officer in the Chivi DA's office, who further claimed that the ruling party is selective in its support for civil society groups; it prefers to promote and support groups that are led by members of the party.

45. At least four focus groups in three districts, when asked who paid for the development of their local areas, indicated that NGOs did. One group in the Masvingo Province was adamant that both the DA and the DC were trying to damage the people's relations with NGOs by insisting that they be informed before a new project is undertaken by the NGOs. In Chipinge, a DC member argued that decentralisation benefits only the DA and his junior officers because they received salaries from government; "... the people get nothing, so NGOs are more legitimate than government".

46. Three focus groups were interviewed in the Kadoma District. Two of them had ten people each while the third one consisted of seven people. The groups were located in three different wards of the district area.

47. The term "sitting pretty" is used in Zimbabwe to denote significant financial and material comfort. The implication was that the councillors were satisfied with their DC allowances, and whatever else they received as community leaders, and were indifferent to the people's needs.

48. Apparently, the DC managed to obtain permission from the relevant authorities in government, and from resettled farmers, for the grazing of CA livestock on RA farms. The major mitigating factor was the drought of 1991/92 which would have resulted in the death of most of the livestock in CAs.

49. One of the focus groups was highly emotional and pointed out that people are told to go to their councillor first; the councillor is the one who can bring their issue before the DC or its administrators. DC administrators denied the charges.

50. Interview with a focus group of seven citizens in the Kadoma District. They further alleged that the DC administrators always claim to be too busy to meet with the ordinary citizens.

51. The same allegation was made in, at least, three other districts included in this study. A surprising feature of the allegation is that in some districts, citizens reported that they had better access to the DA's office than to their DCs.

52. All the three groups in this district agreed that a visit to the DC offices was a "nightmare" in that citizens are endlessly referred to different offices or officials, even for trivial matters which should not take any time to resolve: "It appears, everyone is scared of making a decision because they are afraid of making mistakes", quipped one citizen.

53. Members of this group cited examples of personal experiences with DC officials, some of which were rather difficult to imagine in independent Zimbabwe.

54. The group mentioned some names of "dubious" representatives and all of them were rural businessmen of some local stature. The allegations levelled against these representatives was that they spent most of their time on their own businesses rather than on the affairs of the people.

55. In Maungwe, one focus group alleged that the pre-colonial representatives and council administrators respondent speedily to the people's needs; they were better educated and were elected or appointed on the basis of merit. They contended that current leaders are elected or appointed on partisan basis - on the basis of their support for the ruling ZANU/PF party.

Bibliography

Balogun, M.J., "Local Government and Rural Development: A Critical Review of Efforts, Prospects and Problems", Economic Commission for Africa: Multi-Disciplinary Advisory Group; Paper prepared for the Conference on Rural Development, 21-25 September, 1992, Harare, 1992.

Barkan, J.D. and Chege, M., "Decentralising the State: District Focus and the Politics of Reallocation in Kenya", *The Journal of Modern African Studies; 27.3 431-453.*

Bratton, M., *Beyond Community Development: The Political Economy of Rural Administration in Zimbabwe*; From Rhodesia to Zimbabwe Series No. 6, Mambo Press, Gwelo, 1978.

Ceccarelli, P., "The Territorial Aspects of Decentralization",_____

Chikate. S., "Towards a Unique Local Government System in Zimbabwe"; Paper prepared for the Conference on Rural Development, Harare, 21-25 September, 1992.

Conyers, D., "Decentralization and Development: A Framework for Analysis," *Community Development Journal*; 21.2 88-100, 1986.

Cormack, I., "An Analysis of Rural Development Policy in Zimbabwe"; Paper prepared for the Conference Rural Development, Harare, 21 - 25 September, 1992.

Crook, R. and Manor, J., (1991) *Enhancing Participation and Institutional Performance: Democratic Decentralization in South Asia and West Africa*; A Report to ESCOR, the Overseas Development Administration, on Phase One of a Two Phase Research Project.

De Valk, P. and Wekwete, K.H., (eds) *Decentralization for Participatory*

Planning: Comparing the Experiences of Zimbabwe and Other Anglophone Countries in Eastern and Southern Africa; Avebury, Aldershot, 1990.

Esman, M.J. and Uphoff, N.T., (1984) *Local Organizations: Intermediaries in Rural Development;* Cornell University Press, London, 1984.

Gorvine, A., "The Utilization of Local Government for National Development," *Journal of Local Administration Overseas;* 4.4 225-23, 1965.

Green, D., Ostrom, E., Thompson, J.T. and West, D., *Decentralization: Improving Governance in Sub-Saharan Africa: Synthesis Report,* 1991.

Heath, R., *Service Centres and Service Regions in Rhodesia;* Supplement to *Zambezia* the Journal of the University of Zimbabwe, University of Zimbabwe Publications, Harare, 1990.

Helmsing, A.H.J., "Transforming Rural Local Government: Zimbabwe's Post independence Experience"; *Environment and Planning: Government and Policy;* Vol. 8 87-110, 1990.

Helmsing, A.H.J., Mutizwa-Mangiza, N.D., Gasper, D.R., Brand, C.M., AND Wekwete, K.H., *Limits to Decentralization: Essays on the Decentralization of Government and Planning in the 1980s;* Institute of Social Studies, The Hague, The Netherlands, 1991.

Hyden, G., *No Shortcuts to Progress: African Development Management in Perspective;* Heinemann, London, 1983.

Kalcheim, C., "The Limited Effectiveness of Central Government Control over Local Government," *Planning and Administration;* 7.1 76-86, 1980.

Kasfir, N., "Designs and Dilemmas: An Overview", in Mawhood, P. (ed) *Local Government in the Third World: The Experience of Tropical Africa;* John Wiley and Sons, New York, 1983.

L'Oeil, R.P. (19??) "Main Issues in Decentralization," _____

Laleye, O.M. and Olowu, D., "Decentralization in Africa."

Makumbe, J.Mw., "Economic Crisis and Administrative Incapacity in Zimbabwe," in Kaarsholm, P. (ed) *Institutions, Culture and Change at Local Community Level*; International Development Studies, Occasional Paper No. 3, Roskilde University, Roskilde, Denmark, 1992.

Martinussen, J., (ed) *Development Theory and the Role of the State in Third World Countries*; International Development Studies, Occasional Paper No. 2, Roskilde University Centre, Roskilde, Denmark, 1991.

Mawhood, P., (ed) *Local Government in the Third World: The Experience of Tropical Africa*; John Wiley and Sons, New York, 1983.

Migdal, J.S., *Strong Societies and Weak States: State Society Relations and State Capabilities in the Third World*; Princeton University Press, Princeton, New Jersey, 1988.

Mutizwa-Mangiza, N.D., "Local Government and Planning in Zimbabwe: An Examination of Recent Changes, With Special Reference to the Provincial Regional Level," *Third World Planning Review*; 8.2 153-175, 1986.

Mutizwa-Mangiza, N.D., "Decentralization and District Development Planning in Zimbabwe", *Public Administration and Development*; Vol. 10 1-13, 1990.

Otzen, U., Feige, T., Friedrich, H., Martin, B., Schedel, D. and Wille, S., *Development Management from Below: The Potential Contribution of Co-operatives and Village Development Committees to Self-Management Decentralized Development in Zimbabwe*; German Development Institute, Berlin.

Palley, C., *The Constitutional History and Law of Southern Rhodesia: 1888 - 1965 With Special Reference to Imperial Control*; Clarendon Press, Oxford, 1996.

Republic of Zimbabwe, *The District Councils Act: Chapter 231*; (as amended at 18 April, 1980), Harare, 1980.

Republic of Zimbabwe, "Provincial Councils and Administration in Zimbabwe: A Statement of Policy and a Directive by the Prime Minister"; Ministry of Local Government, Rural and Urban Development, Harare, 1984a.

Republic of Zimbabwe, "Structure of Village Development Committees/ Ward Development Committees and Extension Services"; Ministry of Local Government, Rural and Urban Development, 1984b.

Republic of Zimbabwe, *Rural District Councils Act, Harare,* 1988.

Republic of Zimbabwe, *Guidelines for Provincial Planning*; National Planning Agency, Ministry of Finance, Economic Planning and Development, Harare, 1990.

Republic of Zimbabwe, "Presentation on Decentralized District Development," Ministry of Local Government, Rural and Urban Development, in Conjunction with the Overseas Development Administration, Harare, 1992.

Reynolds, N., "A Charter for the Land: The Rural Structural Adjustment Programme"; Paper prepared for the Association of District Councils of Zimbabwe, Southern Africa Foundation for Economic Research, Harare, 1992.

Roe, E. "Report on the Amalgamation of District Councils and Rural Councils," Centre for Applied Social Sciences Occasional Paper Series - NRM/7/1992: University of Zimbabwe, Harare, 1992.

Rondinelli, D.A., Nellis, J.R. and Cheema, G.S., *Decentralization in Developing Countries: A Review of Recent Experience*; World Bank Staff Working Papers No 581, The World Bank, Washington D.C., 1983.

Smith, B.C. (1985) *Decentralization: The Territorial Dimension of the State*; George Allen and Unwin, London, 1985.

Totemeyer, G., "Public Administration in Third World Countries With Particular Reference to Local Government", Academy Publications A 6; University of Namibia, Windhoek, 1987.

Vosloo, W.B., Kotze, D.A. and Jeppe, W.J.O. (1974) *Local Government in Southern Africa*; Acadermica, Pretoria, 1974.

Walker, D.B., "Decentralization: Recent Trends and Prospects from a Comparative Governmental Perspective," *International Review of Administrative Sciences*; 57.1 113-129, 1991.

Wekwete, K., "The Local Government System in Zimbabwe - Some Perspectives on Change and Development", *Planning and Administration*; Vol. 1 18-27, 1988.

Index

Name Index

Balogun, M.J. 16
Brand, 29, 30, 34, 35, 56

Cliffe, L. 29
Gorvine, A. 52
Cormack, 29
Crook,R. 8, 11, 55
Crook, 55

Day, John 28

Gorvine, 52
Green, D. 13, 15
Guy, G. 17

Helmsing, A.H.J. 25, 26, 34
Hyden, G. 8, 15

Jordan, 22, 25

Kasfir, N. 12, 15

Laleye O.M. 12, 13, 42

Manor, J. 8, 11, 55
Mawhood, P. 7, 10
Migdal, J.S. 52
Mugabe, R.G. 3
Mutizwa-Mangiza, N.D 23, 35

Nkomo, J. 3

Olowu, D. 12, 13, 42
Otzen, U. 9
Patel, 19

Palley, C. 20

Rondinelli, D.A. 7-10 *passim*

Sithole, N. 2
Smith, B.C. 7, 10, 11, 40
Stoneman, C. 29

Wekwete, K.H. 19, 25, 34

Zimbabwe Government 31

Subject Index

Africa decentralisation problems in,
12-17 *see also* decentralisation,
Zimbabwe decentarlisation in; state
in 1 African Advisory Board 20;
Councils 26; *Law & Tribal Court Act
(1969)* 21; Purchase Areas 19, 26

British Government Overseas
Development Administration 4

Chivi District 3

Decentralisation *see also* Zimbabwe
decentarlisation in definition of 7;
democracy and 11 implications on civil
society 64-65; citizens view of 44-49,
67-72, 78; democracy 40-42, 55-61, 78;
organisations 2, government operations
39-41; political process 1; post-colonial
state 76-79; state and politics 52-55;
rationale for, 9-11; types of 8-10
Deconcentration 8, 10
Delegation 8

www.ingramcontent.com/pod-product-compliance
Lightning Source LLC
Chambersburg PA
CBHW062043270326
41929CB00014B/2517